CHINESE REGIONAL COOKING

Gail Weinshel Katz

WEATHERVANE BOOKS
New York

contents

introduction

Why a Regional Chinese Cookbook? Because Chinese cooking has very definite regional origins, mostly because of differences in climate and geography. This book deals with Mandarin, Honan, and Szechwan cooking.

Mandarin cooking was the aristocratic type of cooking done for the royal courts in northern China, in the Peking area. Chefs from all of China were recruited. The most well-known dish from this area is Peking Duck. Mandarin cooking is known for its more mild and subtle seasoning, as compared to other schools of Chinese cooking. You will find such delectable dishes as Shrimp Toast, Chicken Velvet Soup, and Shrimp Peking coming from this area.

Typical dishes from the region of Honan would be delicious Sweet-and-Sour Fish, Lamb with Scallions, and Hot-Pot Cooking (where everyone cooks his own meat and/or fish and vegetables in a boiling pot of broth). This northern region, south of the Peking area, uses liberal amounts of scallions, garlic, and leeks in its cooking. Lamb was introduced into the area by the Mongolians and has remained a favorite.

Szechwan cooking is very spicy and therefore quite distinctive. Szechwan pepper, called fagara, and spices are used generously. The Szechwan area, located in the southwest, is a rich agricultural area that is semi tropical. The story behind the eating of the spicy dishes is that this enables the people to perspire, and thus they are able to live more comfortably in their hot, humid climate. The Szechwan pepper sort of "sneaks up" on your tastebuds. At first it seems tasteless, then *wow*! Spicy Szechwan Pork and Kang Pao Chicken are good examples of this very spicy taste.

There are some recipes in this book that do not have a certain regional distinction and are appropriate for any area.

All types of Chinese cooking use a plentiful amount of vegetables. In fact the amount of vegetables in a dish is usually much more than the amount of meat or fish.

Chinese meals usually end with fresh fruit or a very simple dessert. The Chinese are not great "sweet eaters," either at dessert time or with midday tea.

In any recipes that call for oil and do not specify what kind of oil, please use pure vegetable oil. You will find the results much more satisfying.

If you intend to do a great deal of Chinese cooking, a wok would be a good investment. Yes, you can substitute a skillet, but it is a poor substitute, and the results will not be the same. The conical shape of a wok, with the heat centered at the bottom, makes it ideal for so many things—deep-frying, stir-frying, sautéing, simmering, etc. With the addition of a round cake rack the wok is also ideal for steaming. The wok will withstand very high heat, uses less oil than a regular frying pan, and is ideal for large or small batches of food. And it is fun to cook in a wok!

Remember, in Chinese cooking especially, the food should be as fresh as possible. Don't overcook Chinese food! Each dish should have a pleasant aroma and should be colorful and very pleasing to the eye.

I hope this book will appeal to everyone interested in Chinese cooking. For those who haven't yet ventured into Chinese cooking—please do! Chinese cooking is healthful, fun, and very pleasing to the palate!

guide to unusual ingredients

Agar-agar is gelatin made from seaweed. It is available at Oriental food stores.

Bean curds are custard-like squares sold at Oriental food stores. They are sometimes used as a meat substitute. Store in water in the refrigerator.

Bok choy is a form of Chinese cabbage. It resembles celery, but its stalks are about a foot long. It can be purchased in some supermarkets or specialty markets. You can substitute cabbage.

Brown bean sauce, or "miso," is a thick brown sauce made from fermented soy beans, salt, and flour. It is available in jars or tins at Oriental food stores.

Candied ginger (or crystalized ginger), is sold at supermarkets in boxes or bottles.

Celeriac root is a variety of celery. It can be purchased in some supermarkets or in specialty stores.

Chinese cabbage, or celery cabbage, has a mild celery–cabbage taste. It consists of a solid, oblong head of wide celery-like stalks ending in frilly, pale-green leaves. It is sold in many supermarkets.

Cloud ears is a black, gelatinous fungus that grows on trees. It turns gray-brown when dried and changes to dark brown and expands in size when soaked. When cooked, it adds a crisp, crunchy texture. It will keep dried on the shelf indefinitely.

Coriander is known as Chinese parsley. It is a fresh herb used primarily as a garnish. It can be purchased at Oriental food stores. You can substitute chopped scallions.

Dried chinese mushrooms are available in cellophane bags in some supermarkets or in Oriental stores. Soak in warm water for 20 to 30 minutes before using.

Dried sharks' fins are long, translucent threads of dried cartilage from the fins of sharks. They are sold in Oriental stores.

"Five-spice" powder is a powdered blend of Chinese star anise, fennel, cinnamon, clove, and Szechwan pepper. It can be purchased in Oriental stores in boxes or bulk. Store tightly covered at room temperature. You can substitute allspice.

Gingerroot is a knobby brown root sold by weight in most supermarkets and at Oriental food stores. It will keep in the refrigerator in a covered jar filled with sherry (or water) for several months.

Gingo plum is available at Oriental food stores.

Golden needles is also known as dried lily flower. It resembles a dried yellow flower called tiger lily and is 2 to 3 inches long. Soften in water before cooking, and cut off stem. To store, keep on shelf. It is available at Oriental food stores.

Hoisin sauce is a thick, sweet, brownish-red sauce made from soybeans, flour, sugar, and spices. It can be purchased in cans or bottles at most supermarkets. Refrigerate in a covered jar after opening. It will keep for months.

Leeks are a member of the onion family. They consist of broad leaves that merge into a white bulb at the base. Leeks are sold at most supermarkets.

Lichees are small oval fruits that can be purchased canned at some supermarkets or in Oriental food stores.

Monosodium glutamate (MSG) is a white crystalline powder used to flavor foods.

Oyster sauce is a thick brown sauce made from oysters, salt, and soybeans. It can be purchased in bottles at some supermarkets or in Oriental food stores. Refrigerate after opening.

Rice wine is made from fermented rice. It is available at liquor stores or Oriental food stores. Sherry can be substituted.

Savoy cabbage is a small, light-green cabbage consisting of heavily veined leaves. It is available in some supermarkets and in Oriental food stores. Regular cabbage can be substituted.

Seaweed strips are sold in dehydrated form in Oriental food stores. They are paper-thin and black-purple.

Sesame-seed oil or *sesame oil* is an amber-colored oil with a nutty flavor and is made from roasted sesame seeds. It is available in bottles at most supermarkets in a milder form than the sesame oil sold in Oriental food stores.

Star anise is a licorice-flavored spice that looks like a tiny 8-pointed star. It is sold in Oriental food stores.

Szechwan peppercorns (fagara), are brown peppercorns with a very hot flavor. They are sold in bulk at Oriental food stores. Substitute black peppercorns.

Transparent noodles are also called silver threads, cellophane noodles, and translucent noodles. They are available in some supermarkets or in Oriental food stores.

White rice-wine vinegar is sweeter and milder than American vinegar. It is available in Oriental food stores.

mandarin

appetizers and soups

bacon-wrapped liver appetizers

8 slices bacon, halved crosswise
1 pound chicken livers, halved

1 can (approximately 6 ounces) water chestnuts, drained, sliced vertically
Toothpicks

Lay bacon halves flat. Place chicken-liver half at one end of bacon slice and water-chestnut slice at other end. Roll each toward center; fasten with toothpick through centers of liver and water chestnut.

Preheat wok to 325°F. Place a few appetizers in wok; fry on each side about 5 minutes total or until bacon is browned. Push appetizers up sides of wok; repeat until all are cooked. Makes 16.

shrimp hors d'oeuvres

6 tablespoons oil
1 pound small cleaned shrimp
Salt to taste

1 tablespoon sherry, or to taste

Heat oil; stir-fry shrimp just until color changes. Drain; sprinkle with salt and sherry. Make 6 servings.

shrimp toast

¼ teaspoon sesame-seed oil
¼ teaspoon soy sauce
Pinch of white pepper
Pinch of salt
½ pound uncooked shrimp, cleaned, deveined

8 slices 2-day-old white bread, sliced thin
1 quart vegetable oil

Add sesame-seed oil, soy sauce, pepper, and salt to shrimp; mix thoroughly.

Cut 32 rounds from bread slices. Spread shrimp mixture evenly on 16 rounds. Top each circle with another round; press edges together.

Heat oil in deep pot until very hot. Drop each round into oil; turn to brown evenly. Takes approximately 2 minutes. Drain on paper toweling. Makes 16.

pineapple cocktail barbecue

1 can pineapple chunks (approximately 16 ounces), drained; reserve syrup
1 jar red-cherry preserves or jelly (approximately 10 ounces)
¼ cup catsup
3 whole cloves

1 stick cinnamon
1 teaspoon salt
1 teaspoon cornstarch
2 teaspoons water
1 tablespoon soy sauce
Meatballs, cooked, made from 1 pound ground chuck

Combine pineapple syrup with cherry preserves, catsup, cloves, cinnamon, and salt. Heat to boiling.

Dissolve cornstarch in water until it makes smooth paste. Stir into boiling sauce. Cook until cornstarch thickens and turns clear.

Add pineapple chunks and soy sauce. Pour over meatballs. Keep warm in chafing dish. Serve with toothpicks. Makes 6 to 8 servings.

chicken velvet soup

1 chicken breast, cooked
1 teaspoon salt
2 egg whites, beaten until stiff peaks form
3 cups chicken broth
1 small can cream-style corn
1 tablespoon cornstarch
2 tablespoons cold water
1 teaspoon sherry
2 tablespoons minced beef, cooked

Remove chicken meat from bones; mince. Mix with salt. Fold into egg whites.

Bring broth to boil. Add corn, cornstarch mixed with cold water, and sherry.

Cook 2 minutes over low heat. Stir in chicken mixture. Bring to boil; remove from heat. Garnish each bowl with beef. Makes 6 servings.

mandarin soup

1 tablespoon oil
½ pound pork, trimmed of fat, sliced into thin strips
1 cup chopped celery
½ cup diced carrots
1 cup sliced fresh mushrooms
6 cups chicken broth, homemade or canned
¾ cup finely chopped spinach
MSG to taste
1 egg, beaten
2 tablespoons cornstarch
¼ cup cold water

Heat oil in pot. Sauté pork 10 minutes. Add celery, carrots, and mushrooms; sauté 5 minutes. Stir in chicken broth, spinach, and MSG; bring to boil. Add egg, stirring constantly.

Mix together cornstarch and water. Stir into soup; stir until soup is thickened. Makes 6 servings.

mushroom soup with "sizzling" rice

2 cans (approximately 12 ounces) chicken broth
¼ pound lean pork, finely diced
2 garlic cloves, minced fine
1 tablespoon soy sauce
½ cup sliced fresh mushrooms
¼ cup sliced water chestnuts
¼ cup tiny frozen green peas
"Sizzling" rice (see Index)

Pour broth into saucepan. Add pork, garlic, and soy sauce; simmer 15 minutes. Add mushrooms, water chestnuts, and peas; simmer 2 minutes. Turn into warm heatproof pitcher or bowl. Keep warm in 250°F oven.

Place half of rice into preheated serving bowl. Divide rest of rice among individual soup bowls; pour soup over. Serve rest of rice as accompaniment. Makes 4 or 5 servings.

noodle soup

2 tablespoons dried Chinese mushrooms
½ pound boneless pork
2 tablespoons sherry
2 tablespoons soy sauce
Salt to taste
White pepper to taste
Pinch of ground ginger
1 quart salted water
½ pound transparent noodles
5 ounces bamboo shoots
2 quarts chicken broth
3 tablespoons vegetable oil
1 small can chicken meat, cut into 1-inch squares
5 ounces ham steak, cut into 1-inch squares
½ cup chopped watercress

Soak mushrooms 30 minutes; drain well. Set aside.

Cut pork into 3-inch strips ⅛ inch thick.

Combine sherry, soy sauce, salt, pepper, and ginger in bowl. Add pork. Let stand, covered, 1 hour.

Bring salted water to boil. Add noodles; cook 10 minutes. Drain well; set aside.

Slice mushrooms and bamboo shoots. Add mushrooms, bamboo shoots, and noodles to chicken broth; simmer 2 minutes.

Remove pork from soy-sauce mixture; pat dry. Sauté pork in oil 2 minutes; remove. Add chicken, pork, and ham to broth. Add watercress. Spoon broth into individual soup bowls. Makes 6 servings.

sharks'-fin soup

¾ pound dried sharks' fins
1 tablespoon oil
2 tablespoons sliced fresh gingerroot
¼ cup sliced scallions
1 tablespoon sherry
3 quarts chicken broth
2 tablespoons cornstarch
1 teaspoon soy sauce
¼ cup water
¼ teaspoon MSG
½ pound crab meat

Wash sharks' fins; cover with cold water. Drain; cover with fresh water. Boil 3 hours; drain. Add fresh water; boil 3 hours. Drain; let dry.

Heat oil in large saucepan. Sauté ginger and scallions 3 minutes. Add sherry, 1 quart chicken broth, and sharks' fins. Cook over medium-high heat 15 minutes. Drain any remaining liquid. Add remaining broth; bring to boil.

Mix together cornstarch, soy sauce, water, and MSG. Slowly stir into soup. Stir in crab meat; heat through. Makes about 8 servings.

salads and vegetables

mandarin salad

1 teaspoon soy sauce
¼ cup French dressing
2 cups diced cooked veal
 (ham can be substituted)
¼ cup chopped onion
2 cups fresh bean sprouts

¼ cup sweet pickle relish
¾ cup mayonnaise
½ teaspoon salt
Dash of freshly ground black
 pepper

Combine soy sauce and French dressing. Marinate veal in mixture 45 minutes; chill. Add remaining ingredients; toss lightly. Serve on bed of lettuce. Makes 4 servings.

mandarin-orange gelatin

1 11-ounce can mandarin
 oranges, drained; reserve
 ½ cup liquid
3 tablespoons sauterne
2 3-ounce packages
 orange-flavored gelatin

1 envelope unflavored gelatin
2 cups hot water
1 cup cold water

Combine oranges with 2 tablespoons sauterne.

Combine orange-flavored and unflavored gelatin in large bowl; mix well. Add hot water; stir until gelatin is dissolved. Stir in 1 tablespoon sauterne, reserved mandarin-orange liquid, and cold water. Chill until gelatin is thick and syrupy. Pour about ½ cup gelatin into 1½-quart mold rinsed in cold water. Arrange orange segments petal-fashion in gelatin. Chill until set. Spoon about 1-inch layer thickened gelatin over oranges. Arrange layer of orange segments around edge of mold. Chill until set. Spoon another layer of gelatin over oranges. Repeat layers. Chill until set. Makes 6 servings.

fried bean curd peking-style

1 cup peanut oil
2 bean curds, each cut into 8
 pieces
¼ cup soy sauce
2 tablespoons red-wine
 vinegar

1 tablespoon white vinegar
4 tablespoons chopped
 scallions
1½ teaspoons hot oil

Heat peanut oil to 350°F. Cook bean curds until golden brown.

Mix together soy sauce, red-wine vinegar, white vinegar, scallions, and hot oil in bowl. Serve sauce with bean curds. Makes about 4 servings.

chestnuts with mushrooms

2 tablespoons butter
1 pound small fresh
 mushrooms
18 chestnuts, scalded,
 skinned, simmered in water
 until tender

¼ cup sherry
Salt to taste

Heat butter in skillet. Sauté mushrooms over low heat until soft. Add chestnuts; heat over high heat. Add sherry and salt; cook 1 minute. Makes approximately 4 servings.

pea-pod casserole

1 package frozen pea pods,
  boiled
1 can water chestnuts, sliced
1 can bean sprouts, or fresh
  bean sprouts
1 can cream of mushroom
  soup
1 can onion rings (optional)

Boil pods 2 minutes; drain. Place in casserole dish. Place water chestnuts on top of pods. Next place layer of sprouts. If canned sprouts are used, drain well. Cover with soup. Bake 15 minutes in 350°F oven. Place onion rings on top; heat again, about 5 minutes. Makes 4 servings.

"sizzling" rice

To get the "sizzling" effect, food, rice, and containers must be hot.

1 cup long-grain rice
4 cups water
2 teaspoons salt
Oil for deep frying

At least a day in advance combine rice, water, and salt in 2-quart saucepan. Let stand 30 minutes. Bring to boil; cover. Simmer 30 minutes; drain. Spread evenly on heavily greased cookie sheet. Bake in 250°F oven 8 hours, turning occasionally with spatula. Break crusty rice into bite-size pieces. Can be stored in airtight containers in refrigerator several weeks.

Just before serving time, heat oven to 250°F; warm serving platter.

Pour oil about 2 inches deep in 6-quart saucepan (or deep-fryer). Heat to 425°F. Fry rice, stirring with slotted spoon, until golden brown, approximately 5 minutes. Drain quickly; place in warmed serving platter. Makes 5 or 6 servings.

mandarin-orange gelatin

11

meat and poultry

stir-fried beef and mushrooms

½ pound dried Chinese
  mushrooms
¼ cup flour
1 tablespoon sugar
½ cup sherry
½ cup soy sauce
3 pounds lean steak, cut into
  thin strips
¾ cup oil
1 2-inch slice fresh
  gingerroot, minced
1 cup chopped onions
2 cups beef bouillon
Salt to taste

Soak mushrooms in water 30 minutes. Drain well; set aside.

Combine flour, sugar, sherry, and soy sauce in bowl. Add steak;
marinate 30 minutes, stirring frequently.

Heat ½ cup oil in wok. Stir-fry gingerroot 1 minute. Add beef with
marinade; stir-fry until beef changes color. Remove beef from wok.

Add remaining oil to wok. Add onions; stir-fry until almost tender. Add
mushrooms; stir-fry until soft. Add beef to wok; stir-fry about 2
minutes. Add bouillon. Bring to boil; reduce heat. Add salt. Cover;
cook 2 minutes. Makes 6 to 8 servings.

stir-fried beef and mushrooms

beef slices peking

3 tablespoons soy sauce
1 tablespoon sherry

Blend soy sauce and sherry in a deep bowl.

1 pound lean beef, sliced paper-thin	2 garlic cloves, minced
Marinade	½ teaspoon powdered ginger
1 cup oil	2 tablespoons soy sauce
2 tablespoons flour	⅛ teaspoon ground anise
2 leeks, sliced thin	½ cup beef broth
	1 teaspoon cornstarch

Add beef to marinade; coat well. Cover; let stand 1 hour.

Heat oil in large skillet. Thoroughly drain beef slices on paper toweling. Sprinkle with flour. Add to hot oil; deep-fry 3 minutes. Remove meat with slotted spoon; drain. Set aside; keep warm.

Pour 4 tablespoons hot oil into another skillet. Throw away rest of frying oil. Reheat oil. Add leeks and garlic; cook 5 minutes, stirring. Add meat slices. Season with ginger, soy sauce, and anise. Pour in broth. Cover; simmer over very low heat 1 hour. At end of cooking time, bring to quick boil.

Blend cornstarch with small amount cold water. Add to skillet; stir constantly until sauce is slightly thickened and bubbly. Correct seasoning, if necessary. Serve immediately. Makes 2 servings.

beef slices peking

mandarin liver

This is an excellent dish. Very good with rice.

1 pound liver (pork, baby beef, or calves)
2½ tablespoons flour
5 tablespoons safflower oil
Salt to taste
Pepper to taste
3 tablespoons soy sauce
2 tablespoons Chinese rice wine or sherry
2 large onions, sliced thin
1 cup beef bouillon (from cubes)
1 red pepper, cut into strips
1 green pepper, cut into strips
½ pound savoy cabbage, cut into strips
6 ounces fresh bean sprouts
1 small can bamboo shoots (approximately 6 ounces)

Pat liver dry with paper towels; cut into thin slices. Coat with flour.

Heat oil in heavy skillet. Add liver; brown on all sides; remove. Season to taste with salt and pepper. Set aside; keep warm.

Add soy sauce, wine, and onions to pan drippings; simmer 5 minutes. Pour in beef bouillon. Add red and green peppers and cabbage; simmer 10 minutes. Vegetables should still be crisp. Add bean sprouts, bamboo shoots, and liver; heat through. Serve immediately. Makes 4 servings.

mandarin liver

beef balls

1 pound lean ground beef
¼ cup dry bread crumbs
1 egg, beaten
2 tablespoons flour
¼ cup cold water
1¼ teaspoons salt

½ cup oil
¼ cup soy sauce
½ cup boiling water
1 pound spinach, washed,
   stems discarded

Mix together beef, bread crumbs, egg, flour, cold water, and 1 teaspoon salt. Shape into 8 balls.

Heat oil in wok or skillet. Brown beef balls in hot oil. Drain off all oil; discard all but 2 tablespoons. Add soy sauce and boiling water. Cover; cook over low heat 35 minutes.

Heat reserved oil in separate skillet. Sauté spinach and ¼ teaspoon salt 2 minutes. Combine with meat balls; cook 3 minutes. Makes 3 or 4 servings.

bean sprouts with chicken

1½ pounds shredded chicken
   meat
2½ teaspoons rice wine or
   sherry
1½ teaspoons salt
1 egg white
1 tablespoon cornstarch

Oil for frying
12 ounces fresh bean sprouts
½ teaspoon MSG
½ teaspoon sesame oil
1 teaspoon cornstarch
1 teaspoon water

Mix chicken with 1½ teaspoons wine, salt, and egg white. Coat with 1 tablespoon cornstarch. Deep fry chicken in oil in wok or deep skillet until color changes. Remove from oil; drain.

Leave 1 tablespoon oil in pan. Stir-fry bean sprouts. Add chicken, MSG, 1 teaspoon wine, sesame oil, and cornstarch mixed with water. Stir until all ingredients are heated through. Makes 5 to 6 servings.

mandarin chicken

This is very good with steamed rice.

3 tablespoons soy sauce
½ teaspoon dried dillweed
1 whole chicken breast,
   skinned, boned, cut into
   bite-size pieces
3 tablespoons peanut oil
½ cup thinly sliced celery

1 8-ounce can water
   chestnuts, drained, sliced
   thin
1 11-ounce can
   mandarin-orange sections,
   drained, liquid reserved
1 tablespoon cornstarch

Combine 2 tablespoons soy sauce and dillweed. Pour over chicken; let stand 30 minutes.

Heat 1 tablespoon oil in wok or large skillet. Add celery and water chestnuts. Stir-fry 2 minutes or until celery turns bright green. Remove from wok; set aside.

Heat 2 tablespoons oil in wok. Add chicken mixture; stir-fry about 3 minutes or until chicken is very tender. Return vegetables to wok.

Blend liquid from mandarin-orange sections with cornstarch and 1 tablespoon soy sauce. Slowly stir into wok; cook until bubbly. Add orange sections; cook 1 minute or until heated through. Makes 2 servings.

peking duck

Delicious!

4- to 5-pound duck
6 cups water
¼ cup honey
4 slices fresh gingerroot, about 1 inch diameter and ⅛ inch thick
2 scallions, sliced

Wash duck thoroughly with cold water; dry. Tie cord tightly around neck skin; suspend duck in airy place to dry skin (about 3 hours).

Bring water to boil. Add honey, gingerroot, and scallions. Lower duck by its string into boiling liquid; moisten duck's skin thoroughly, using spoon. Suspend duck by its cord until dry (about 3 hours).

sauce

¼ cup hoisin sauce
1 tablespoon water
1 teaspoon sesame-seed oil
2 teaspoons sugar

Combine all sauce ingredients in small pan; stir until sugar dissolves. Bring to boil; simmer 3 minutes. Set aside to cool.

12 scallion brushes
Mandarin Pancakes (see Index)

Cut scallions to 3-inch lengths; trim off roots. Stand each scallion on end; make 4 intersecting cuts 1 inch deep into each stalk. Repeat at other end. Place scallions in ice water; refrigerate until cut parts curl.

Preheat oven to 375°F.

Untie duck; cut off loose neck skin. Place duck breast-side-up on rack; set in roasting pan. Roast 1 hour; lower heat to 300°F. Turn duck on its breast; roast 30 minutes. Raise heat to 375°F. Return duck to its back; roast 30 minutes. Transfer to carving board. With small, sharp knife, using your fingers, remove crisp skin from breast, sides, and back of duck. Cut skin into 2 × 3-inch rectangles; arrange in single layer on platter. Cut wings and drumsticks from duck; cut all meat from breast and carcass. Slice meat into pieces 2½ inches long and ½ inch wide; arrange on another platter.

Serve duck with Mandarin Pancakes, sauce, and scallion brushes. Dip scallion brush into sauce; brush pancake with it. Scallion is placed in middle of pancake with piece of duck skin and piece of meat. Pancake is rolled around pieces and eaten like a sandwich. Makes about 6 servings.

oriental chicken

4 ounces almonds, slivered
3 tablespoons peanut oil
¾ cup chopped onion
4 chicken breasts, boned, sliced thin
2 cans (approximately 6 ounces each) sliced bamboo shoots, drained
1 can water chestnuts, drained, sliced
1 cucumber, unpeeled, sliced thin

½ cup chicken stock
2 teaspoons sherry
¼ teaspoon ground ginger
1 teaspoon soy sauce
½ teaspoon cornstarch
1 tablespoon cold water
Salt to taste
Freshly ground pepper to taste

Brown almonds in 400°F oven about 10 minutes. Watch closely. Set aside.

Pour oil into large frying pan or wok; heat to medium-high heat. Add onion; cook until limp. Remove onion from pan (push up side, if using wok).

Add chicken to pan; toss gently about 1 minute. Add bamboo shoots and water chestnuts; toss gently 1 minute. Add cucumber; cook 1 minute.

Combine stock, sherry, ginger, and soy sauce. Add to pan; cook 1 minute.

Combine cornstarch and water in small dish. Stir slowly into hot mixture. Season with salt and pepper. Cook until liquid is thickened. While cooking, return onions to mixture. Serve chicken with rice and browned almonds. Makes 4 servings.

sesame chicken

1 chicken, 2 to 2½ pounds, washed, dried, disjointed
Flour, seasoned with salt and freshly ground black pepper
2 eggs, beaten
2 tablespoons milk

1 cup flour
½ cup sesame seeds
½ teaspoon salt
¼ teaspoon freshly ground black pepper
Peanut oil for frying
Light Cream Sauce

Dust chicken with seasoned flour.

Mix together eggs and milk. Dip floured chicken into milk mixture.

Mix 1 cup flour with sesame seeds, salt, and pepper. Roll chicken in mixture. Deep fry in oil until light brown and tender. Serve with Light Cream Sauce. Makes 4 servings.

light cream sauce

4 tablespoons butter
4 tablespoons flour
½ cup half-and-half
1 cup chicken stock

½ cup whipping cream
Onion salt to taste
Freshly ground black pepper to taste

Melt butter over low heat. Add flour; blend, stirring constantly, several minutes.

Mix together half-and-half, stock, and whipping cream. Gradually add to butter and flour, stirring constantly. When mixture is smooth, stir in onion salt and pepper.

Let cook over hot water in double boiler about 15 minutes; stir occasionally.

chicken with dates

1 chicken, approximately 3 to 3½ pounds
Salt
Pepper
Curry powder
2 tablespoons oil
1 medium onion, chopped
2 green peppers, cut into thin strips
1 cup beef bouillon
½ pound rice
1 teaspoon cornstarch
12 dates, pitted, cut into halves
1 cup yogurt
3 tablespoons toasted sliced almonds

Divide chicken into 8 pieces. Remove all except wing and leg bones. Rub chicken with salt, pepper, and curry powder.

Heat oil in heavy skillet. Add chicken; cook until golden on all sides. Add onion; cook until golden. Add green peppers. Pour in bouillon; simmer over low heat 30 minutes.

Meanwhile cook rice according to package directions.

Remove chicken from sauce; keep warm. Strain sauce.

Blend cornstarch with small amount cold water. Slowly stir into sauce; cook until thick and bubbly. Add dates.

Beat yogurt with fork; stir into sauce. If necessary, correct seasonings. Heat through, but do not boil. Spoon rice into bowl or platter; arrange chicken on top. Pour sauce over chicken; top with almonds. Makes 4 or 5 servings.

chicken velvet

Delicious!

Meat from 2 chicken breasts, minced
2 teaspoons cornstarch
¼ cup cold water
Pinch of salt
3 egg whites, beaten until stiff peaks form
Vegetable oil for frying
2 ounces snow-pea pods, cut in half
1 tablespoon oil

sauce

1 teaspoon cornstarch
1 teaspoon cold water
½ cup chicken broth
1 tablespoon sherry
1 tablespoon vegetable oil

Mix chicken with cornstarch, water, and salt. Fold mixture into egg whites. Drop by teaspoonfuls into hot oil; cook until lightly browned. Drain on paper toweling.

Sauté pea pods in 1 tablespoon oil until well coated.

Mix cornstarch with cold water in small saucepan until smooth. Add rest of ingredients; bring to boil. Add sauce and chicken to snow peas. Bring to boil. Makes 2 servings.

chicken with dates

pork with peas

marinade

2 tablespoons soy sauce
**2 teaspoons rice wine or
 sherry**
⅛ teaspoon MSG
1 egg white
1 teaspoon cornstarch
Salt
White pepper

Thoroughly combine soy sauce, wine, MSG, egg white, and cornstarch.
Season to taste with salt and white pepper.

Marinade
**12 ounces lean pork, cut
 crosswise into thin strips**
4 ounces frozen peas
8 tablespoons oil
**½ cup hot beef broth (made
 from cubes)**
Salt
Sugar
1 leek, cut into julienne strips
1 clove garlic, minced
**4 ounces canned sliced
 mushrooms**

pork with peas

20

**4 ounces canned bamboo
 shoots**
**1 preserved gingo plum,
 sliced**
**1 tablespoon rice wine or
 sherry**
1 tablespoon cornstarch
2 teaspoons soy sauce
2 tablespoons oyster sauce
White pepper
Pinch of ground ginger

Pour marinade over pork; cover. Let marinate 30 minutes.

Meanwhile thaw peas.

Heat 2 tablespoons oil in small saucepan. Add peas; pour in broth.
Season to taste with salt and sugar; cook 5 minutes. Drain peas,
reserving cooking liquid; keep warm.

Heat 3 tablespoons oil in large saucepan. Add leek, garlic, mushrooms,
bamboo shoots, and gingo plum. Cook 5 minutes, stirring constantly.
Set aside; keep warm.

Heat 3 tablespoons oil in skillet. Add meat with marinade; cook 3
minutes or until meat is browned, stirring occasionally. Add meat and
peas to large saucepan with vegetables. Pour in wine and reserved
cooking liquid; bring to boil.

Blend cornstarch with soy sauce and oyster sauce; stir until slightly
thickened and bubbly. Season to taste with salt, pepper, ginger, and
sugar. Serve immediately. Makes 2 servings.

fish and seafood

poached fish mandarin-style

½ teaspoon shredded fresh gingerroot
2 scallions, cut into 1-inch pieces
1 tablespoon soy sauce
1 tablespoon peanut oil
1 tablespoon sherry
1 whole fresh fish (bass, flounder, sole, butterfish, whitefish), cleaned, washed, dried inside and out (about 1½ to 2 pounds)

Mix together ginger, scallions, soy sauce, oil, and sherry. Rub mixture all over fish, inside and out.

Place water in bottom of wok; put fish on rack in wok, making sure water does not touch fish. Steam over high heat about 20 minutes or until fish is done. Makes 3 or 4 servings.

mandarin oranges with shrimp

This is so simple, but so good!

2 teaspoons sherry
1 teaspoon cornstarch
½ pound shrimp, cleaned
Oil for cooking
½ cup drained canned mandarin-orange segments
¼ teaspoon sugar
¼ teaspoon salt
Boiled rice

Mix together sherry and cornstarch. Marinate shrimp in mixture 5 minutes.

Heat oil in wok or skillet, enough to cover bottom. Stir-fry shrimp just until color changes. Add mandarin-orange segments, sugar, and salt; stir-fry just until heated through, no more than 1 minute. Serve with rice. Makes 2 servings.

oyster chow mein

¼ cup butter
1 pint oysters, drained, liquid reserved
3 tablespoons butter
1 medium onion, chopped
½ cup chopped green pepper
¾ cup diagonally sliced celery
1 cup sliced fresh mushrooms
3 tablespoons flour
2 cups fresh bean sprouts
2 tablespoons soy sauce
Salt to taste
Freshly ground black pepper to taste
Chow-mein noodles

Melt ¼ cup butter in skillet. Cook oysters over medium heat until edges curl.

Melt 3 tablespoons butter in another skillet. Sauté onion, green pepper, celery, and mushrooms until tender. Stir in flour. Add oysters and liquid, adding enough water to make ¾ cup. Cook, stirring constantly, until thickened. Add bean sprouts, soy sauce, salt, and pepper. Heat through, stirring gently. Serve over chow-mein noodles. Makes 3 or 4 servings.

22

shrimp with peas

2 quarts water
2 cups frozen peas
1 tablespoon vegetable oil
1 small slice fresh gingerroot
¼ cup diagonally sliced green
   onions
1 cup uncooked shrimp,
   deveined, cut in half
Salt to taste
Freshly ground black pepper
   to taste
1 teaspoon cornstarch
1 tablespoon cold water
½ teaspoon sesame-seed oil

Bring water to boil. Add peas; bring to boil again. Drain peas; set aside.

Preheat wok (or skillet); coat bottom and sides with oil. Rub gingerroot on bottom and sides of wok, then discard. Stir-fry onions quickly. Add shrimp; stir-fry until just cooked. Shrimp will turn pink when done. Add salt and pepper.

Blend cornstarch with cold water. Stir this and peas into shrimp mixture. Add sesame oil; stir. Serve immediately. Makes 4 servings.

shrimp peking

1 pound shrimp, cleaned,
   shelled
½ teaspoon salt
1 egg, beaten
2 tablespoons cornstarch
3 tablespoons peanut oil
2 tablespoons finely chopped
   scallions
1 small slice gingerroot,
   chopped
2 cloves garlic, minced
2 tablespoons soy sauce
2 tablespoons chicken broth
1 tablespoon dry sherry
2 teaspoons chopped red
   pepper
1 tablespoon vinegar
2 teaspoons sugar
4 water chestnuts, sliced

Sprinkle shrimp with salt. If shrimp are very large, cut in half.

Mix together egg and cornstarch to make batter. Coat shrimp evenly with batter.

Heat oil in wok (or frying pan) over medium-high heat. Stir-fry shrimp 3 minutes, separating them. Remove shrimp from wok. Drain; keep warm.

Place scallions and ginger in wok; stir-fry 1 minute. Add garlic, soy sauce, broth, sherry, red pepper, vinegar, and sugar. Cook, stirring constantly, until mixture comes to boil. Return shrimp to wok. Add water chestnuts; stir-fry 2 minutes. Serve immediately. Makes 2 servings.

miscellaneous

shrimp egg foo yung

1 cup chopped fresh bean
sprouts
¼ cup chopped white onions
¼ cup chopped fresh
mushrooms
¼ cup finely chopped cooked
shrimp

1 teaspoon soy sauce
Pinch of salt
4 eggs
¼ cup crisp noodles
Oil for frying

Mix together sprouts, onions, mushrooms, shrimp, soy sauce, and salt. Add eggs; mix. Mix in noodles. Shape mixture into hamburger-size patties. Heat oil (small amount) in frying pan. Cook each patty about 2 minutes on each side. Can be served with Sweet-and-Sour Sauce (see Index). Makes 4 servings.

oriental scrambled eggs

3 tablespoons chopped
scallions
2 tablespoons butter
½ cup sliced water chestnuts
2 cups fresh bean sprouts
6 eggs

½ teaspoon salt
¼ teaspoon freshly ground
black pepper
2 teaspoons soy sauce (or to
taste)

Sauté scallions in butter until tender. Add water chestnuts and bean sprouts, mixing gently.

Combine eggs with salt, pepper, and soy sauce; beat slightly. Pour egg mixture over vegetables in pan. Cook over medium heat, stirring occasionally, until eggs are done as desired. Makes 3 or 4 servings.

mandarin pancakes

These are traditionally served with Peking Duck (see Index). As a shortcut use leftover duck that has a crisp skin. These are really very easy to make!

2 cups sifted all-purpose flour
¾ cup boiling water
1 to 2 tablespoons sesame-seed oil

Make well in sifted flour in bowl; pour water into it. Mix with wooden spoon until soft dough. Knead dough gently on lightly floured surface 10 minutes. It should be smooth. Let rest under damp kitchen towel 15 minutes. On lightly floured surface roll dough to about ¼ inch thick. With 2½-inch glass cut as many circles as you can. Use scraps of dough, kneading them again and cutting out more circles. Brush half of circles lightly with sesame-seed oil. Place unoiled circle on top of oiled one. Flatten each pair with rolling pin to diameter of about 6 inches. Turn once to roll both sides, trying to keep circular shape. Cover pancakes with dry towel.

Heat 8-inch ungreased skillet to high heat. Reduce heat to moderate. Cook pancakes one at a time, turning them as little bubbles and brown specks appear. Cook about 1 minute on each side. As each pancake is cooked, gently separate halves; stack on plate. Makes about 24.

honan

appetizers and soups

salted chicken

1½ tablespoons salt
1¼ teaspoons MSG
1 tablespoon rice wine
2 small slices gingerroot
2 scallions, cut into 1-inch
  pieces

1 whole chicken, 2½ to 3
  pounds
Cold water
1 cup chicken stock
¼ teaspoon salt
1 tablespoon sesame oil

Mix together salt, 1 teaspoon MSG, wine, gingerroot, and scallions.
Rub chicken with mixture; let stand 30 minutes. Place chicken in pot;
cover with cold water. Bring to boil; simmer 40 minutes over medium
heat. Remove from pot; chill. Remove skin; cut into pieces
approximately 2 inches long and 1 inch wide.

Mix together stock, ¼ teaspoon salt, ¼ teaspoon MSG, and sesame oil.
Pour over chicken. Garnish with additional scallions if desired. Makes
12 servings.

chicken wings in oyster sauce

3 tablespoons oil
2 cloves crushed garlic
8 chicken wings, each divided
  into 3 parts

2 tablespoons soy sauce
3 tablespoons oyster sauce
1 tablespoon sugar
½ cup water

Preheat wok. Coat bottom and sides with oil. Rub bottom and sides
with garlic; discard garlic. Add middles and tips of wings; brown on
both sides. Add rest of wing pieces; brown.

Mix together soy sauce and oyster sauce; stir into chicken. Stir in sugar
and water. Cover wok; cook over medium-low heat 15 minutes. Makes
4 servings.

sweet-and-sour spareribs

5 tablespoons soy sauce
2 tablespoons sherry
2 cloves garlic, minced
1 teaspoon sugar
1½ pounds spareribs

1 tablespoon cornstarch
1 tablespoon vinegar
1 teaspoon cornstarch
Oil for cooking

Combine 3 tablespoons soy sauce, 1 tablespoon sherry, garlic, and 1
teaspoon sugar; blend well.

Have butcher cut crosswise through bones of spareribs at about 1- to
1½-inch intervals. Cut bones apart. Pour soy-sauce mixture over
spareribs. Let stand at room temperature 1 hour; stir occasionally. Blend
in 1 tablespoon cornstarch.

Blend together 2 tablespoons sugar, 2 tablespoons soy sauce, 1
tablespoon sherry, vinegar, and 1 teaspoon cornstarch together in
saucepan. Cook over medium heat, stirring constantly, until thickened.
Set aside.

Heat approximately 3 inches oil in deep pot.

Drain marinade from spareribs. Add portion of meat at a time to hot oil;
cook until well browned. Drain on paper toweling. Place cooked
spareribs into cooked sauce; coat well. Cover; chill. Serve spareribs at
room temperature. Makes about 24 to 28 pieces.

abalone appetizer

1 teaspoon grated fresh
gingerroot
1 tablespoon soy sauce

1 tablespoon sherry
1 can abalone, drained, cut
into bite-size pieces

Mix together ginger, soy sauce, and sherry. Pour over abalone.
Refrigerate several hours. Makes 5 or 6 servings.

scallops honan-style

1 cup soy sauce
1 tablespoon lemon juice
2 teaspoons finely chopped
fresh gingerroot

2 tablespoons sugar
¼ teaspoon MSG
1 pound scallops, cut into
bite-size pieces

Combine soy sauce, lemon juice, ginger, sugar, and MSG in large
saucepan; bring to boil. Add scallops; cook over medium-high heat
until all liquid has evaporated. Makes approximately 25 appetizers.

crab soup

2 tablespoons oil
½ pound crab meat
¼ teaspoon salt
2 medium tomatoes, coarsely
chopped
1½ teaspoons chopped fresh
gingerroot

5 cups chicken broth
2 eggs, beaten
1½ tablespoons vinegar
1½ tablespoons sherry
1½ tablespoons soy sauce
3 scallions, sliced

Heat oil in large pot. Sauté crab meat, salt, tomatoes, and ginger 5
minutes. Add chicken broth; cook over low heat 10 minutes.

Beat eggs. Add vinegar, sherry, and soy sauce. Slowly pour into soup.
Stir in scallions; let soup simmer about 3 minutes. Makes 4 to 6
servings.

hot-and-sour soup

¼ cup cloud ears
¼ cup golden needles
¼ pound pork, shredded into
1½-inch-long strips
3 tablespoons cornstarch
2 teaspoons sherry
½ cup water
3 tablespoons white-wine
vinegar (or to taste)
White pepper to taste

½ teaspoon hot oil
2 teaspoons sesame-seed oil
4 cups chicken stock
Salt to taste
1 tablespoon soy sauce
2 bean curds, each cut into 8
pieces
1 egg, beaten
2 scallions, chopped

Soak cloud ears and golden needles in hot water about 15 minutes or
until noticeably increased in size; drain. Shred cloud ears. Cut golden
needles in half.

Combine pork with 1 tablespoon cornstarch and sherry.

Mix 2 tablespoons cornstarch with water; set aside.

Combine vinegar, pepper, hot oil, and sesame oil in bowl; set aside.

Bring chicken stock, salt, and soy sauce to boil in large soup pot. Add
pork; boil 1 minute. Add cloud ears, golden needles, and bean curds;
boil 1 minute. Add cornstarch mixture; stir until thickened. Lower heat.
Add vinegar mixture. Taste; adjust seasoning if necessary. Slowly stir in
egg. Garnish with scallions. Makes 5 or 6 servings.

salads and vegetables

asparagus salad

This is a nice accompaniment to a Chinese meal.

1 tablespoon soy sauce
½ teaspoon red-wine vinegar
2 teaspoons sesame oil
1 teaspoon sugar
1 pound asparagus, tough ends broken off, sliced into 2-inch lengths

Combine soy sauce, vinegar, oil, and sugar; stir until sugar dissolves.
Bring pot of water to boil. Drop asparagus into water; cook 1 minute.
Drain; rinse with cold water. Toss asparagus with soy-sauce mixture;
chill. Makes about 4 to 5 servings.

honan-style chicken salad

1 pound chicken meat, shredded (leftover chicken is fine)
3 cucumbers, cut into matchstick pieces
1 leek, white part only, cut into small thin pieces
1 tablespoon minced fresh gingerroot

2 tablespoons soy sauce
2 tablespoons red-wine vinegar
2 tablespoons sugar
1 teaspoon crushed red pepper
1 tablespoon sesame oil
1 tablespoon sesame seeds, toasted in hot frying pan

Mix chicken with cucumbers; place in serving dish. Sprinkle with leek
and gingerroot; chill in refrigerator.

Mix together soy sauce, vinegar, sugar, red pepper, and oil; blend
thoroughly. Stir in sesame seeds. Just before serving, toss with chicken
mixture. Makes about 4 servings.

deep-fried crispy noodles

1 5-ounce package fine egg noodles
Vegetable oil

Place noodles in large saucepan in enough water to cover; bring to boil.
Cook, stirring occasionally, 5 minutes; drain well.

Fill deep-fat fryer half full with oil; heat to 350°F. Drop noodles into
basket in oil; cook 2 minutes. Remove from oil; drain well on paper
toweling.

Heat oil to 375°F. Return noodles to fryer; cook until golden brown and
crisp. Drain well on paper toweling; separate noodles if necessary.
Makes 4 to 5 cups noodles.

soft-fried noodles with mushrooms

1 5-ounce pakage fine egg
  noodles
2 tablespoons safflower oil
1 cup bamboo shoots
1 cup sliced fresh mushrooms
1 cup sliced almonds
½ cup chicken broth
3 tablespoons soy sauce
Salt to taste

Cook noodles in large pot in boiling, lightly salted water 8 minutes; drain well.

Heat oil in wok or skillet over low heat. Add noodles; stir-fry 4 minutes. Stir in bamboo shoots, mushrooms, and almonds; mix thoroughly. Stir in broth, soy sauce, and salt. Reduce heat to low; simmer, covered, 20 minutes or until liquid is almost absorbed. Makes 8 servings.

deep-fried crispy noodles
soft-fried noodles with mushrooms

fried rice with mushrooms

fried rice with mushrooms

½ cup sliced dried
   mushrooms
¼ cup olive oil
¼ cup sliced green onions
2 cups long-grain rice
4 cups chicken stock
⅛ teaspoon dry mustard
1 tablespoon soy sauce
½ cup white bean curd, cut
   into cubes
¼ cup safflower oil
¾ cup cooked fresh green
   peas
Radish flowers for garnish

Soak mushrooms in cold water 5 minutes; drain well.

Heat olive oil in wok or deep skillet over medium heat. Add onions; stir-fry until onions are limp and transparent. Add rice; stir-fry until rice is golden. Add 1 cup stock and mustard; stir-fry 2 to 3 minutes or until liquid is absorbed. Add 1 cup stock and soy sauce; stir-fry until liquid is absorbed. Add 1 cup stock; reduce heat to low. Stir in bean curd; cook, stirring occasionally, until liquid is absorbed. Add remaining stock, safflower oil, peas, and mushrooms. Cover; cook, stirring occasionally, about 20 to 25 minutes or until rice is tender. Spoon into serving dish; garnish with radish flowers. Makes 10 servings.

meat and poultry

beef in oyster sauce

½ teaspoon salt
¾ teaspoon baking soda
4 tablespoons water
3 teaspoons rice wine
½ teaspoon baking powder
¾ tablespoon cornstarch
2 teaspoons soy sauce
8 ounces lean beef, cut into bite-size slices
3½ teaspoons oil

Oil for deep frying
6 scallions, cut into 2-inch slices
2 small slices fresh gingerroot
1½ teaspoons oyster sauce
¼ teaspoon MSG
¼ teaspoon sugar
½ teaspoon sesame oil
½ teaspoon cornstarch

Mix together salt, baking soda, 3 tablespoons water, 1½ teaspoons rice wine, baking powder, ¾ tablespoon cornstarch, and 1 teaspoon soy sauce. Coat beef slices with mixture. Add 1½ teaspoons oil. Let stand 1½ hours.

Deep-fry beef in hot oil until color changes. Remove; drain on paper toweling.

Sauté scallions and gingerroot in 2 tablespoons oil. Add beef, 1½ teaspoons rice wine, oyster sauce, 1 teaspoon soy sauce, MSG, sugar, sesame oil, and cornstarch mixed with water. Stir-fry quickly until heated through. Makes 2 or 3 servings.

beef pot roast

1 teaspoon salt
½ teaspoon freshly ground black pepper
2 teaspoons brown-gravy sauce

¼ cup soy sauce
2 tablespoons margarine
1 5-pound beef pot roast
1 medium onion, sliced
1 cup water

Mix together salt, pepper, brown-gravy sauce, and soy sauce. Rub into meat. Let sit 30 minutes.

Brown meat in melted margarine in Dutch oven. Place rack under roast in Dutch oven. Add onion and water. Cover; cook slowly on stove or in 350°F oven approximately 3½ hours or until tender. Add more water if necessary. (There should be about 1 inch water in pot.) Turn meat occasionally during cooking. Serve with gravy. Makes about 8 servings.

gravy

6 tablespoons drippings from roast
6 tablespoons flour
2 tablespoons soy sauce
1 teaspoon brown-gravy sauce
½ teaspoon salt

Dash of freshly ground black pepper
½ cup cold water
1½ cups hot water

Melt drippings; blend in flour. Add soy sauce, brown-gravy sauce, salt, pepper, and cold water; mix thoroughly. Stir in hot water. Cook, stirring constantly, until smooth and thickened.

lamb with garlic

2 pounds shoulder lamb chops
Water for boiling
16 cloves garlic
1 leek, cut into 2-inch slices
6 small slices fresh gingerroot
2 cloves star anise
2 teaspoons whole anise pepper
6 tablespoons soy sauce
3 tablespoons sherry
Oil
2 teaspoons cornstarch
1 tablespoon water

Parboil lamb in enough water to cover; discard water. Place lamb, garlic, leek, ginger, star anise, whole anise pepper, soy sauce, and sherry in large pot with water to cover. Cover; bring to boil over high heat. Reduce heat to low; simmer until tender (about 1 hour). Remove lamb; drain liquid. Reserve liquid and garlic.

Heat oil to medium heat. Deep-fry lamb until crisp.

Heat 1 cup reserved liquid. Add cornstarch mixed with water; stir until thickened.

Place lamb and garlic on serving platter; pour gravy over lamb. Makes 2 main-course servings.

oriental meatballs

These are a favorite of ours!

2 pounds lean ground beef
2½ teaspoons salt
¼ teaspoon freshly ground
   black pepper
1 egg, beaten
2 tablespoons flour
Small amount freshly ground
   black pepper
½ cup peanut oil
12 ounces canned chicken
   broth
3 tablespoons cornstarch
2½ teaspoons soy sauce
½ cup vinegar
½ cup light corn syrup
5 medium green peppers, cut
   into sixths
8 slices canned pineapple,
   quartered
10 maraschino cherries
   (optional)

Combine beef, 1 teaspoon salt, and ¼ teaspoon pepper. Shape into small meatballs.

Combine egg, flour, ½ teaspoon salt, and small amount pepper. Beat until smooth.

Heat oil and 1 teaspoon salt in large frying pan.

Gently place meatballs in batter, 1 or 2 at a time; fry in hot oil, browning well on all sides. Remove meatballs from pan; drain remaining oil.

Blend ½ cup broth with cornstarch. Add remaining broth, soy sauce, vinegar, and corn syrup. Cook over medium heat, stirring constantly, until thick and clear. Add green peppers, pineapple, and cherries. Lower heat; cook slowly about 10 minutes. Pour over meatballs. Serve with rice. Makes 6 servings.

honan lamb chops

2 tablespoons oil
4 shoulder lamp chops, about ¾ inch thick
1 medium onion, diced
½ cup diced green pepper
½ cup diced celery
1 can (approximately 5 ounces) bamboo shoots, sliced
1 pound fresh bean sprouts
½ teaspoon salt
¼ teaspoon freshly ground black pepper
1½ teaspoons soy sauce
1 tablespoon cornstarch
1 tablespoon water
1 medium tomato, cut into wedges

Preheat wok or skillet to 350°F. Pour in oil. Add lamb; cook until browned on both sides. Add onion, green pepper, and celery.

Drain bamboo shoots. Add liquid to wok. Cover; simmer on low heat about 30 minutes or until lamb is tender. Add sprouts, bamboo shoots, salt, and pepper.

Mix together soy sauce, cornstarch, and water until smooth. Stir into lamb mixture. Add tomato; cook 2 minutes or until sauce is thickened. Makes 4 servings.

marinated lamb

3 pounds boneless lamb, cut into ½-inch cubes
1 cup cider vinegar
½ cup minced onions
3 garlic cloves, minced
2 teaspoons salt
1 teaspoon ground coriander
1 teaspoon ground cumin
½ teaspoon saffron
½ teaspoon dried ground chili peppers
1 teaspoon ground ginger
4 tablespoons oil
½ cup water
Boiled rice

Marinate lamb in vinegar 30 minutes; drain well.

Grind together onions, cloves, salt, coriander, cumin, saffron, chili peppers, and ginger to make paste. Roll lamb in mixture; let stand 30 minutes.

Heat oil in pan. Brown lamb. Stir in water. Cover; cook over low heat 45 minutes or until lamb is very tender. Serve with rice. Makes 6 servings.

lamb with scallions

1 pound boneless lamb, fat trimmed, sliced ⅛ inch thick, cut into strips
½ teaspoon five-spice
1 egg white
3 thin slices fresh gingerroot
3 cloves garlic, minced
3 teaspoons cornstarch
5 teaspoons soy sauce
6 tablespoons sherry
2 tablespoons water
12 whole scallions
2 tablespoons oil

Mix lamb in bowl with five-spice, egg white, ginger, garlic, 1 teaspoon cornstarch, and 1 teaspoon soy sauce. Let stand 20 minutes.

Blend rest of cornstarch, soy sauce, sherry, and water; set aside.

Cut white part of scallions in half crosswise. Cut green tops into 1-inch pieces; set aside.

Heat oil in wok or skillet to high heat. Add meat mixture; cook, stirring constantly, until meat is slightly browned. Remove from wok.

Add cornstarch–soy-sauce mixture and white parts of onion to wok. Cook, stirring constantly, until thickened. Add meat and green tops of onions; stir until simmering. Makes 3 or 4 servings.

stir-fried lamb

This is good with boiled rice.

1 tablespoon soy sauce
1 teaspoon light brown sugar
3 tablespoons chicken stock
1 tablespoon gin
¼ teaspoon powdered
   five-spice
1 pound boned lamb, cut into
   thin bite-size pieces
2 tablespoons peanut oil
2 teaspoons minced garlic
Salt to taste
3 leeks, white part only,
   sliced into 1-inch pieces

Mix together soy sauce, sugar, stock, gin, and five-spice. Marinate lamb in mixture 30 minutes.

Heat wok to high heat. Add oil, garlic, and salt; stir about 30 seconds or until garlic odor becomes strong. Add lamb and marinade; stir-fry 2 to 3 minutes. Add leeks; stir-fry 1 minute. Makes 3 or 4 servings.

pork cubes in sweet-and-sour sauce

2½-pound slice pork
   shoulder, bone removed,
   meat cut into 1-inch cubes
2 cups water
½ teaspoon salt
4 tablespoons soy sauce
2 tablespoons sherry

Put meat into large pot. Add water, salt, and soy sauce. Bring to boil on high heat. Turn heat to low; cover pot. Simmer about 1 hour or until tender. Drain off meat broth; reserve. Skim off fat. Add sherry to broth; set aside.

sweet-and-sour sauce

⅓ cup sugar
4 tablespoons cornstarch
4 tablespoons cider vinegar
⅓ cup pineapple juice
Broth from meat
⅔ cup pineapple chunks (1
   8-ounce can)

Blend sugar, cornstarch, vinegar, and pineapple juice in saucepan; mix until smooth. Slowly stir in meat broth. Stir over medium-high heat until sauce is thick and clear, approximately 8 minutes.

Pour sauce over pork cubes. Add pineapple chunks; mix carefully. Makes 6 servings.

paper-wrapped chicken

These are very easy to make and are delicious!

1 pound chicken meat, sliced
  very thin
2 tablespoons soy sauce
1 tablespoon dry sherry
½ teaspoon brown sugar
½ teaspoon salt
1 scallion, sliced thin

1 teaspoon grated fresh
  gingerroot
16 pieces cooking parchment;
  if unavailable, use foil,
  approximately 4 inches
  square
Vegetable oil for frying

Combine chicken, soy sauce, sherry, brown sugar, salt, scallion, and ginger. Marinate 30 minutes. Divide chicken mixture into 16 portions. Wrap each portion in piece of cooking parchment; fasten well.

Heat oil in wok to 375°F. Deep-fry packages a few at a time 3 minutes. Drain on paper toweling; keep hot. Serve wrapped to keep in juices. Each is unwrapped just before eating. Makes 4 servings.

chicken with walnuts

1 pound white chicken meat,
  cut into 1-inch cubes
1 teaspoon salt
1 teaspoon sugar
1 tablespoon soy sauce
3 tablespoons sherry
2 tablespoons cornstarch
1 egg, beaten

½ cup peanut oil
1 cup walnuts
2 teaspoons minced fresh
  gingerroot
3 garlic cloves, minced
½ cup boiling water
MSG to taste
1 cup sliced bamboo shoots

Combine chicken in bowl with salt, sugar, soy sauce, and sherry; mix well. Let stand 30 minutes. Drain; reserve marinade. Dip chicken pieces into cornstarch, then into egg.

Heat oil in wok or deep skillet; brown walnuts. Remove walnuts; pour off all but 2 tablespoons oil. Brown chicken, ginger, and garlic. Add water, MSG, bamboo shoots, and marinade. Cover; cook over low heat 10 minutes. Add walnuts; mix through. Makes 4 servings.

chicken go wan

2 whole chicken breasts,
  boned, cut into ½-inch
  cubes
¾ cup soy sauce
2 cups long-grain rice
4½ cups chicken stock
1 teaspoon MSG
1 cup sliced fresh mushrooms

Combine chicken and soy sauce in mixing bowl; let stand 1 to 2 hours to marinate.

Combine rice, stock, MSG, and mushrooms in Dutch oven; mix lightly. Spoon chicken and soy sauce over top. Cover; cook over low heat approximately 30 minutes or until chicken and rice are tender. Makes 4 to 6 servings.

deep-fried sweet-and-sour chicken

2 tablespoons cornstarch
2 tablespoons soy sauce
1 teaspoon salt
2 eggs
Oil for cooking
1 4-pound cooked chicken,
  boned, skinned, meat cut
  into 1-inch cubes

Combine cornstarch and soy sauce; mix well.

Combine salt and eggs in mixing bowl; beat with whisk until light. Stir in cornstarch mixture until just mixed.

Heat oil in deep-fryer to 375°F or until small ball of flour mixed with water dropped into oil floats to top immediately.

Dip chicken into egg mixture; drain slightly. Drop chicken, several cubes at a time, into oil. Fry until lightly browned; drain on paper toweling. Place chicken in individual serving dishes. Spoon Sweet-and-Sour Sauce over chicken. Makes 4 to 6 servings.

sweet-and-sour sauce

¾ cup sugar
2 tablespoons soy sauce
1 tablespoon dry white wine
3 tablespoons wine vinegar
3 tablespoons catsup
2 tablespoons cornstarch
½ cup water

Combine sugar, soy sauce, wine, vinegar, and catsup in saucepan; bring to boil.

Dissolve cornstarch in water; add to sauce. Cook over low heat, stirring, until sauce has thickened. Makes 1 to 1¼ cups.

oriental chicken with vegetables

¼ cup soy sauce
¼ cup chicken broth
2 whole chicken breasts,
  skinned, boned, meat cut
  into bite-size pieces
4 tablespoons peanut oil
1 clove garlic, minced
2 small yellow squash, sliced
  thin

1 medium zucchini, sliced
  thin
6 ounces snow-pea pods,
  fresh or frozen
½ pound fresh mushrooms,
  sliced
Boiled rice

Mix soy sauce with broth in shallow bowl. Marinate chicken in mixture at least 1 hour.

Heat 2 tablespoons oil in wok until sizzling. Add garlic; cook 2 minutes.

Drain chicken; reserve marinade. Cook chicken in wok, stirring constantly, 2 minutes. Remove from wok; keep warm.

Add 2 tablespoons oil to wok; heat. Add squash and zucchini; stir-fry until coated with oil. Push to one side. Add pea pods and mushrooms; toss to coat with oil. Add chicken and soy-sauce mixture; cover. Reduce heat; simmer 5 minutes or until vegetables are tender but still crispy. Serve with rice. Makes 4 servings.

deep-fried sweet-and-sour chicken

fish and seafood

sweet-and-sour fish

3 to 3½ pounds fish fillets
  (carp, bass, or fish of your
  choice)
4 tablespoons finely chopped
  onions
2 teaspoons chopped fresh
  gingerroot
½ teaspoon MSG

Pinch of salt
¼ teaspoon freshly ground
  black pepper
1 teaspoon soy sauce
1 teaspoon sherry
½ cup cornstarch (more if
  needed)
Fat for deep frying

Sprinkle fish with onions, gingerroot, MSG, salt, pepper, soy sauce, and sherry. Let stand 30 minutes. Roll in cornstarch; let stand 10 minutes.

Heat fat in deep-fryer or deep skillet over medium-high heat. Fry fish 10 to 15 minutes or until done. Drain fish. Serve with sauce. Makes 4 servings.

sweet-and-sour sauce

¾ cup cider vinegar
1 tablespoon cornstarch
1 green pepper, cut into
  julienne strips
1 carrot, peeled, cut into
  julienne strips
2 teaspoons chopped fresh
  gingerroot

4 scallions, sliced into ½-inch
  pieces
2 tablespoons sweet pickle
  relish
Salt to taste
¼ cup sugar

Mix together all ingredients. Cook over low heat, stirring constantly, until thickened.

fried shrimp with pineapple

1 cup sifted all-purpose flour
1 teaspoon baking powder
1 teaspoon salt
1 egg, beaten
½ cup beer
Fat for deep frying
1 pound raw shrimp, shelled,
  deveined

1 tablespoon cornstarch
1 tablespoon sugar
4 tablespoons vinegar
½ cup pineapple juice
1 cup pineapple chunks

Sift flour, baking powder, and ½ teaspoon salt into bowl. Beat in egg and beer.

Heat fat in deep-fryer or deep skillet to medium high.

Dip shrimp in batter, coating well on all sides. Fry in hot fat until nicely browned. Drain; keep warm.

Mix cornstarch with sugar, ½ teaspoon salt, and vinegar. Add pineapple juice; cook over low heat, stirring constantly, until thickened.

Arrange shrimp on serving platter. Place pineapple chunks around shrimp; pour sauce over all. Makes 4 servings.

tuna casserole

1 small can tuna
½ cup diced onion
½ cup diced celery

8 ounces fresh bean sprouts
¼ cup diced green pepper
Soy sauce to taste

Drain tuna; mix with remaining ingredients. Place in casserole. Bake in 350°F oven 25 minutes. Add additional soy sauce if desired. Makes 2 or 3 servings.

miscellaneous

hot-pot cooking

"Hot-Pot Cooking" is a one-pot meal that is cooked at the table, similar to our Swiss fondue. The hostess presents an artistically arranged platter of selected meats, seafood, and vegetables. These are passed around. Each diner selects from the platter and cooks his or her meal in a pot of chicken broth, which is later eaten as soup with rice or noodles added to it. A "hot-pot" meal might consist of the following:

Chicken broth
White rice or thin noodles
Selection of meats, seafood, and vegetables
Sauces for dipping the meats, seafood, and vegetables

Some suggestions are:

Flank steak, cut into thin slices
Boneless lean lamb
Boned chicken breast
Shrimp, shelled, deveined
Scallops
Oysters
Celery cabbage
Spinach
Fresh mushrooms
Pea pods
Hot mustard sauce (dry mustard mixed to a paste with water)
Soy sauce
Chinese oyster sauce
Hoisin sauce
Teriyaki sauce
Chinese plum sauce

For 4 people, select 6 to 8 foods (variety of meat, seafood, and vegetables).

fruit cocktail

This is a pretty dessert and a nice combination of textures.

4 cups water
3 tablespoons sugar
1 small can mandarin oranges
3 pineapple slices, quartered
6 canned water chestnuts,
  sliced
12 strawberries, halved

Place water and sugar in saucepan; heat until sugar dissolves. Remove from heat; cool. Add oranges, pineapple, water chestnuts, and strawberries. Mix gently; chill. Makes 2 or 3 servings.

szechwan

appetizers and soups

cucumber hors d'oeuvres

2 tablespoons oil
3 small red chili peppers, seeded, cut into very thin slices
4 medium to large cucumbers, cut into 2-inch lengths, quartered, seeded
1 teaspoon soy sauce
2 tablespoons sugar
¼ teaspoon salt
1 tablespoon vinegar

Heat oil in skillet. Add chili peppers; stir-fry 4 seconds. Add cucumbers; stir-fry 30 seconds. Add soy sauce, sugar, and salt; stir until well blended. Refrigerate at least 24 hours; remove cucumbers from liquid. Sprinkle with vinegar. Makes 6 servings.

sandie's chicken wings

1 10-ounce bottle soy sauce
2 teaspoons freshly grated gingerroot
2 cloves garlic, minced
⅓ cup brown sugar
1 teaspoon dark mustard
24 chicken wings
Garlic powder

Mix together soy sauce, ginger, garlic, brown sugar, and mustard; blend well. Marinate chicken in mixture 2 hours or longer. Drain wings; reserve marinade. Bake 1½ hours at 350°F, turning and basting with marinade frequently. Sprinkle with garlic powder. Place under broiler to get crispy a minute or two just before serving. Makes 8 to 12 servings.

cabbage and bean-thread soup

2 ounces pork, thinly sliced into small pieces
1¼ teaspoons soy sauce
1 teaspoon cornstarch
½ ounce transparent (cellophane) noodles
2 tablespoons oil
1 teaspoon salt
1 teaspoon MSG
3 cups water
¼ cup thinly sliced Chinese cabbage
½ cup thinly sliced cucumber
1 tablespoon chopped green onion
¼ teaspoon freshly ground black pepper
½ teaspoon seasame-seed oil

Mix pork with 1 teaspoon soy sauce and cornstarch.

Place noodles in bowl with enough hot water to cover. Let stand 5 minutes.

Sauté pork in oil over moderate heat until tender: remove.

Add salt and MSG to water; bring to boil. Add noodles, pork, cabbage, and cucumber.

Mix together onion, pepper, sesame oil, and ¼ teaspoon soy sauce. Add to soup; mix well. Heat through. Makes 6 servings.

cabbage and ham soup

½-pound sliced ham, rind removed, boned, cut into ½-inch cubes
6 cups cold water
1 teaspoon salt
1 Chinese cabbage, leaves separated, washed

Place ham and bone into deep pot. Add water. Sprinkle in salt. Cover: bring to boil over high heat. Turn heat to simmer: cook about 25 minutes.

Place leaf stalks of cabbage together; slice crosswise into thin slices. Add to ham mixture. Heat to boiling: simmer 10 minutes. Serve immediately. Makes 6 servings.

celery soup

1 heaping tablespoon dried Chinese mushrooms
2 small celeriac roots, with green tops (celery stalks can be substituted)
4 tablespoons oil
½ pound pork shoulder, cut into 1½-inch-long, ½-inch-thick strips
2 small onions, minced
1 clove garlic, minced
3 cups hot chicken broth, from cubes or homemade
2 quarts salted water
1 ounce Chinese transparent noodles
2 tablespoons soy sauce
⅛ teaspoon ground ginger

Soak mushrooms in cold water 30 minutes.

Cut off celeriac tops; set aside. Brush celeriac roots under running cold water. Peel; cut into ½-inch cubes.

Heat oil in saucepan. Add pork; brown on all sides, stirring constantly, about 3 minutes. Add onions, garlic, and celeriac root; cook 5 minutes.

Drain mushrooms; cut in halves, or quarters if very large. Add to saucepan. Pour in broth. Cover; simmer over low heat 25 minutes.

Meanwhile bring salted water to boil in another saucepan. Add noodles. Remove from heat immediately; let stand 5 minutes. Drain noodles.

Five minutes before end of cooking time of soup, add coarsely chopped celeriac tops. Season to taste with soy sauce and ground ginger.

Place noodles in soup tureen or 4 individual Chinese soup bowls. Pour soup over noodles. Serve immediately. Makes 4 servings.

celery soup

wonton soup

dumpling dough

**4 ounces flour
Salt
1 tablespoon milk
2 tablespoons oil
1 small egg**

filling

**4 ounces fresh spinach,
  chopped
4 ounces ground pork
½ tablespoon soy sauce
⅛ teaspoon ground ginger**

soup

**5 cups chicken broth
2 tablespoons chopped chives**

Stir together flour and salt in bowl. Add milk, oil, and egg. Knead dough until smooth. Roll out dough on floured board until paper-thin. Cut into 3-inch squares. Cover with kitchen towel while preparing filling.

Thoroughly wash spinach; remove coarse stems. Place in bowl; barely cover with boiling water. Let stand 3 minutes; drain well. Coarsely chop. Add pork, soy sauce, and ginger; blend thoroughly. Place 1 teaspoon filling on each dough square, giving filling lengthy shape. Fold over dough from one side; roll up jelly-roll fashion. Press ends of roll together to seal.

Bring broth to boil. Add wontons; simmer over low heat 20 minutes. Spoon into bowls. Garnish with chives. Makes 6 servings.

wonton soup

vegetables

bean sprouts and vinegar

1 teaspoon Szechwan
   peppercorns
3 tablespoons oil
1½ pounds fresh bean
   sprouts
¼ cup thin strips green
   pepper

1 teaspoon salt
½ teaspoon sugar
½ teaspoon MSG
2 teaspoons vinegar

Fry peppercorns in oil until fragrant. Remove peppercorns; discard. Add remaining ingredients to same pan; stir-fry until heated through. Serve immediately. Makes 4 or 5 servings.

stir-fried bok choy

2 tablespoons peanut oil
2 cloves garlic, minced fine
1 pound bok choy, sliced diagonally
Salt to taste
Freshly ground black pepper to taste

Heat oil in wok or skillet. Add garlic. Add bok choy; stir-fry until coated with oil and heated through. Sprinkle with salt and pepper; mix thoroughly. Serve immediately. Makes 4 servings.

chow choy

This is a very unusual and tasty vegetable dish.

¼ cup olive oil
1 teaspoon cayenne pepper
1 clove garlic, minced
Salt to taste
4 cups chopped Chinese cabbage
2 tablespoons soy sauce
2 tablespoons red-wine vinegar
1 teaspoon MSG
1 teaspoon sugar
3 scallions, chopped
1 tablespoon cornstarch
2 tablespoons cold water

Heat oil in wok or large skillet over medium heat. Stir in pepper, garlic, and salt. Add cabbage and soy sauce; stir-fry 2 minutes. Add vinegar, MSG, sugar, and scallions; stir-fry 1 minute.

Mix cornstarch with cold water until smooth; stir into cabbage mixture. Stir-fry about 2 minutes or until mixture is lightly browned. Makes 4 servings.

eggplant szechwan-style

1 large eggplant, peeled, cut in half lengthwise, cut into 2½-inch sections
Oil for deep frying
4 ounces ground pork
3 tablespoons oil
2 teaspoons hot soybean paste
2 tablespoons chopped scallions
1 tablespoon chopped fresh gingerroot
2 tablespoons chopped garlic
1 teaspoon soy sauce
1 teaspoons rice wine
1 teaspoon sugar
1 teaspoon MSG
1 teaspoon dark vinegar
1 teaspoon cornstarch
1 teaspoon water

Deep-fry eggplant until tender. Remove; drain on paper toweling.

Stir-fry pork in 3 tablespoons oil. Add soybean paste, scallions, ginger, and garlic; stir-fry 1 minute. Add eggplant, soy sauce, rice wine, sugar, MSG, and vinegar.

Mix cornstarch with water; stir into eggplant mixture until thickened. Makes 4 or 5 servings.

spicy seaweed

4 ounces seaweed strips
3 cups boiling water
1 tablespoon salt
1½ teaspoons finely chopped scallions
1 tablespoon finely chopped fresh gingerroot
1½ teaspoons finely chopped hot red pepper
½ teaspoon salt
½ teaspoon MSG
⅓ teaspoon dark vinegar
½ teaspoon sesame oil

Place seaweed in boiling water. Add 1 tablespoon salt. When water comes to boil, remove seaweed. Rinse in cold water; drain well.

Mix together remaining ingredients. Add seaweed; toss. Makes about 6 servings.

red and green pepper pot

This is so easy, and very delicious!

¼ cup butter
3 red peppers, cut into rings
3 green peppers, cut into rings
6 yellow onions, peeled, cut into wedges
12 tomatoes, stem ends cut off, cut into wedges
Salt to taste
Freshly ground black pepper to taste

Melt butter in skillet. Add peppers and onions; sauté over low heat 10 minutes, stirring frequently. Add tomato wedges. Season with salt and pepper. Cook 10 minutes, stirring frequently. Makes 6 servings.

red and green pepper pot

meat and poultry

spiced beef

2 tablespoons peanut oil
1 pound boneless stewing
  beef, cut into 1-inch cubes
2 tablespoons dry sherry
3 tablespoons soy sauce
1 teaspoon sugar
3 scallions, cut into 1-inch
  pieces
1 cup cold water
¼ teaspoon star anise

Heat oil in skillet over high heat. Add beef; cook, turning constantly, until browned on all sides. Add sherry, soy sauce, and sugar; mix well. Cook 2 minutes. Stir in scallions. Add water; bring to boil. Reduce heat to medium; cover. Cook 15 minutes; stir occasionally. Stir in star anise. Reduce heat to low; cook 20 minutes. Makes 3 servings.

cashew chicken

2 tablespoons oil
½ teaspoon salt
1 cup sliced chicken breast
  meat
¾ cup pea pods
½ cup bamboo shoots
½ cup sliced fresh
  mushrooms
1 cup chicken broth
½ cup cashew nuts (or as
  desired)
¼ teaspoon sugar
¼ teaspoon MSG
½ teaspoon cornstarch
1 teaspoon water

Coat preheated wok with oil (swirl around). Sprinkle in salt. Stir-fry chicken 2 minutes. Add pea pods, bamboo shoots, mushrooms, and chicken broth. Cover wok; cook 2 minutes. Carefully stir in nuts, sugar, and MSG.

Mix cornstarch with water; stir into chicken mixture until thickened. Makes 4 servings.

kang pao chicken
(spicy chicken)

12 ounces boned chicken, cut
  into ½-inch squares
1 egg white
2 teaspoons cornstarch
2 tablespoons brown bean
  sauce
1 tablespoon hoisin sauce
2 teaspoons sherry
1 teaspoon sugar
1 tablespoon white rice-wine
  vinegar
2 tablespoons water
2 teaspoons minced garlic
1 cup peanut oil
1¼ teaspoons crushed red
  pepper (or as desired)
½ cup roasted peanuts

Combine chicken with egg white and cornstarch in bowl.

Mash bean sauce in separate bowl. Add hoisin sauce, sherry, sugar, vinegar, water, and garlic.

Heat wok over high heat. Add oil. When oil is very hot, add chicken; stir 30 seconds or until chicken changes color. Remove from wok; set aside.

Drain off all but 2 tablespoons oil. Reheat wok. When oil is very hot, add red pepper; stir 25 seconds or until pepper darkens. Add chicken, bean-sauce mixture, and peanuts to wok; stir 1 minute or until heated through. Makes 2 or 3 servings.

barbecued chicken

Whichever way you choose to serve this, you will enjoy it!

¼ cup soy sauce
2 garlic cloves, minced
2 teaspoons salt
¼ teaspoon freshly ground
   black pepper
1 teaspoon five-spice

1 teaspoon sugar
2 tablespoons oil
1 roasting chicken,
   approximately 4 pounds,
   whole, washed, dried

Mix together soy sauce, garlic, salt, pepper, five-spice, sugar, and oil. Rub into inside and outside of chicken. Let stand 1 hour. Place chicken on rack in shallow roasting pan. Roast in 425°F oven 2½ hours or until chicken is tender and nicely browned. Turn and baste often.

To serve, chicken can be cut up with bones left on (American-style), or meat can be taken off bones and cut into pieces about 1 inch square (Chinese-style). Makes about 4 servings.

chicken with sweet peppers

2 whole chicken breasts,
   boned, cut into 1-inch
   pieces
2 cloves garlic, pressed
4 tablespoons olive oil
3 tablespoons soy sauce
½ teaspoon salt
¼ teaspoon freshly ground
   black pepper
2 teaspoons cornstarch
2 green peppers, seeds and
   membrane removed, cut
   into 1-inch pieces

1 red pepper, seeds and
   membrane removed, cut
   into 1-inch pieces
8 green onions, cut into
   ½-inch pieces
3 celery stalks, cut into
   ½-inch pieces
¼ teaspoon sugar
¼ cup cold water

Combine chicken, garlic, 1 tablespoon oil, 2 tablespoons soy sauce, salt, pepper, and 1 teaspoon cornstarch in mixing bowl; mix well. Let marinate at least 30 minutes.

Heat 3 tablespoons oil in wok. Add peppers; stir-fry 3 minutes. Add onions and celery; stir-fry 2 minutes. Using slotted spoon, remove vegetables; keep warm.

Place chicken in hot oil in wok; stir-fry 5 minutes.

Combine 1 tablespoon soy sauce, 1 teaspoon cornstarch, sugar, and water. Pour over chicken. Add vegetables; combine carefully, cooking over low heat about 2 minutes or until heated through. Makes about 4 servings.

cornish hen with hot sauce

1 Cornish hen, about 1½
   pounds
1 teaspoon finely chopped
   gingerroot
1 teaspoon finely chopped
   scallion
1 tablespoon soy sauce

½ teaspoon MSG
1 teaspoon sesame oil
1 teaspoon dark vinegar
1 tablespoon Tabasco sauce
1 teaspoon sugar
Parsley for garnish

Cook hen in boiling water until tender. Remove; cool. Cut meat into bite-size pieces. Place on serving platter.

Mix together rest of ingredients; pour over chicken. Garnish with parsley if desired. Makes 2 servings.

salt duck

This recipe seems like a lot of steps, but it is actually very simple and quite tasty.

3 tablespoons Szechwan
  peppercorns
½ cup kosher salt
1 duck, approximately 5
  pounds

3 tablespoons sherry
½ cup chopped coriander for
  garnish (optional)

Mix peppercorns with salt. Toast mixture in pan over low heat, shaking pan occasionally. When peppercorns have nice aroma, remove from heat; cool. Crush peppercorns.

Wipe duck with paper towels; rub inside and outside with salt mixture. Cover; refrigerate overnight. Before cooking duck, rinse thoroughly with cold water. To cook duck, put in heatproof bowl. Rub outside of duck with sherry. Cover bowl; place on trivet in bottom of large pot. Put water in pot, enough to reach halfway up bowl. Bring water to boil; lower heat to simmer. Cook 1 hour and 45 minutes, adding water if necessary. Let duck reach room temperature. Remove from bowl; drain excess liquids from inside duck into bowl. Chop duck meat into bite-size pieces. Arrange on serving platter. Pour liquid over duck; refrigerate 2 hours before serving. Garnish with coriander. Makes 4 servings.

szechwan duck

4 slices fresh gingerroot,
  minced
4 scallions, chopped fine
2 tablespoons salt
1 tablespoon Szechwan
  peppercorns
1 duck, 4 to 5 pounds,
  washed, cleaned

1 quart vegetable oil
Lotus-Leaf Rolls
2 tablespoons salt mixed with
  1 teaspoon peppercorns,
  roasted in oven 10 minutes

Mix together gingerroot, scallions, salt, and peppercorns. Rub inside and outside of duck with mixture. Press on breastbone of duck; break to flatten it. Refrigerate overnight. Steam duck 2 hours; cool thoroughly.

Heat oil in wok or deep pot to 375°F. Deep-fry duck about 7 minutes or until golden brown and crisp.

Serve with Lotus-Leaf Rolls. Diner takes meat off bones (comes off easily with chopsticks), dips it into roasted salt-and-peppercorn mixture, then makes sandwich on Lotus-Leaf Roll. Makes 4 servings.

lotus-leaf rolls

1 cup flour
2 teaspoons sugar
2 teaspoons baking powder

½ cup milk (water can be
  substituted)
Oil

Mix flour with sugar and baking powder. Slowly add milk; stir with fork until soft dough. Knead 5 minutes. Cover with clean, dry cloth; let stand 15 minutes. Knead 2 minutes. Make about 1 inch diameter roll from dough. Cut into pieces about 1 inch thick. Brush with small amount oil; fold over. Use fork to make indentations all around edge. Steam 8 minutes over medium-high heat.

crispy duck

1 duck, about 4 pounds
6 small slices fresh gingerroot
3 tablespoons salt
4 scallions, chopped fine
1 teaspoon Szechwan
  peppercorns

1 tablespoon rice wine or
  sherry
4 star anise
3 tablespoons soy sauce
Oil for deep frying

Coat duck well with mixture of gingerroot, salt, scallions, peppercorns, rice wine, and star anise. Let stand 30 minutes. Steam duck about 1 hour or until very tender. Remove; rub with soy sauce. Deep-fry until golden brown. Cut meat into bite-size pieces. Arrange on serving platter. Makes about 3 servings.

bean curd with pork

½ pound ground pork
3 tablespoons soy sauce
1 tablespoon hoisin sauce
1 teaspoon Tabasco sauce
2 tablespoons cornstarch
¼ teaspoon sesame-seed oil

2 tablespoons chopped
  scallions
1 tablespoon oil
½ cup diced green peppers
4 pieces bean curd

Mix pork with soy sauce, hoisin sauce, Tabasco sauce, cornstarch, and sesame-seed oil.

Quickly fry scallions in 1 tablespoon oil. Add pork mixture, green pepper, and bean curd. Stir-fry 10 to 15 minutes or until pork is done. Makes 4 servings.

spicy pork

1½ pounds lean pork, your
  favorite cut
3 tablespoons peanut oil
3 cloves garlic, minced
2 small slices fresh
  gingerroot, minced
½ cup 2-inch pieces leek
½ cup sliced bamboo shoots

½ cup small pieces red or
  green sweet pepper
¼ teaspoon crushed red
  pepper
3 tablespoons water
1½ teaspoons sugar
4 tablespoons hoisin sauce
Boiled rice

Boil pork 25 minutes; cool. Slice into bite-size pieces; set aside.

Heat oil in wok or skillet over high heat. Cook garlic and ginger 1 minute. Add leek, bamboo shoots, and sweet pepper; mix well. Stir in red pepper. Add pork slices; mix through. Add water; bring to boil. Add sugar and hoisin sauce; stir quickly 1 minute or until sauce coats ingredients. Serve with rice. Makes 4 servings.

pork with vegetables

This goes well with steamed rice.

1 cup thinly sliced raw pork
2 cloves garlic, crushed
½ cup slivered carrots
1 tablespoon soy sauce
2 tablespoons sherry
2 tablespoons oil

4 scallions, chopped fine
½ cup thinly sliced celery
½ teaspoon dry mustard
1 pound raw spinach,
  chopped into bite-size
  pieces

Place pork, garlic, and carrots into bowl.

Mix together soy sauce and sherry. Pour over pork mixture; marinate in refrigerator overnight.

Heat oil in wok or large skillet; stir-fry meat mixture approximately 4 minutes or until pork is cooked. Add scallions, celery, mustard, and spinach; stir-fry 2 minutes. Makes 2 or 3 servings.

meat platter szechwan

7 tablespoons oil
6 ounces fresh mushrooms, sliced
½ pound tomatoes, peeled, sliced
½ pound green peppers, cut in half, seeds removed, cut into julienne strips
1½ pounds lean pork, cut into 2-inch-long julienne strips
Salt
¼ teaspoon ground ginger
½ pound onions, minced
1 clove garlic, minced
2 tablespoons sherry
1 cup hot beef broth (made from cubes)
1 tablespoon soy sauce
2 tablespoons cornstarch
4 tablespoons water

Heat 4 tablespoons oil in skillet. Add mushrooms, tomatoes, and green peppers. Cook 5 minutes; set aside.

Heat 3 tablespoons oil in another skillet. Add meat strips. Season to taste with salt and ginger, stirring constantly. Brown 10 minutes. Add onions and garlic; cook 5 minutes. Pour in sherry. After 1 minute pour in broth and soy sauce. Add vegetable mixture. Cover; cook over medium heat 25 minutes.

Blend cornstarch with water; stir in. Cook until thickened and bubbly. Serve immediately on preheated platter. Makes 4 servings.

meat platter szechwan

fish and seafood

oysters in ginger sauce

1 pint oysters, preferably
  small ones
⅛ teaspoon five-spice powder
1½ teaspoons cornstarch
4 teaspoons soy sauce
3 tablespoons sherry
10 whole scallions
2 tablespoons oil
4 thin slices fresh gingerroot

Mix oysters with five-spice powder, 1 teaspoon cornstarch, and 1 teaspoon soy sauce; set aside.

Blend ½ teaspoon cornstarch, 3 teaspoons soy sauce, and sherry; set aside.

Cut white part from scallions; cut each in half crosswise. Cut green parts into 1-inch sections.

Heat oil in wok or large frypan over high heat. Add ginger and white parts of onions; cook and stir about 1 minute. Remove onion from pan; set aside.

Spread out oysters in pan. Lower heat to medium; cook until oysters are just firm, turning once. Remove oysters from pan.

Cook drippings until browned. Blend in cornstarch–sherry mixture; cook and stir until thickened. Blend in whites and greens of onions and oysters; heat through until mixture simmers. Makes 2 servings.

sesame salmon

3 salmon steaks, cut into
  thirds
1 green pepper, cut into thin
  strips
1 leek, cut into thin strips
2 cloves garlic, minced
½ red chili pepper, minced
1 tablespoon sesame seeds
2 teaspoons vinegar
1 tablespoon sesame-seed oil
2 tablespoons soy sauce
2 teaspoons sugar
3 tablespoons water

Combine all ingredients; let stand 45 minutes.

Preheat oven to 400°F.

Wrap each piece of fish in foil; bake until tender, about 20 to 25 minutes. Makes 3 servings.

curried shrimp

1 pound fresh shrimp,
  shelled, cleaned
Juice of 1 lemon
1 egg white
1 tablespoon cornstarch
2 cups sesame-seed or vegetable oil
1 tablespoon dried Chinese
  mushrooms
1 can (approximately 6
  ounces) bamboo shoots
1 medium onion, chopped
½ teaspoon ground ginger
1 green pepper, sliced thin
2 teaspoons curry powder
1 teaspoon sugar
2 tablespoons soy sauce
8-ounce can tiny peas, drained
2 tablespoons rice wine or
  sherry

Sprinkle shrimp with lemon juice.

Blend egg white and cornstarch; coat shrimp with mixture.

Heat oil in heavy, deep skillet or deep-fryer. Fry shrimp 2 to 3 minutes; remove with slotted spoon. Set aside; keep warm.

Break mushrooms into small pieces; cover with boiling water. Let soak 15 minutes.

Drain bamboo shoots; reserve liquid. Cut shoots into thin strips.

Pour 2 tablespoons oil used for frying into skillet. Add bamboo shoots and onion; cook until transparent. Pour in ½ cup reserved liquid from bamboo shoots. Season with ground ginger. Add green pepper; cook 5 minutes. Pepper should be crisp. Add curry powder, sugar, and soy sauce.

Drain soaked mushrooms. Add mushrooms, peas, and shrimp to skillet. Fold in carefully; heat through.

Heat wine in small saucepan; pour over dish just before serving. Makes 4 servings.

curried shrimp

53

general
(no specific region)

appetizers and soups

sandie's easy vegetarian egg rolls

These egg rolls are delicious. Try them!

Vegetables such as:

Bean sprouts	**Green pepper**
Bok choy	**Scallions**
Cabbage	**Oil for frying**
Carrots	**Soy sauce to taste**
Celery	**Garlic powder**
Fresh mushrooms	**Peanut butter**
Onions	

Use as many above vegetables as you wish, in amounts you desire. Shred or finely chop all vegetables. Stir-fry quickly in small amount of oil. Add soy sauce, garlic powder, and some peanut butter. Fill purchased egg roll or wonton skins (appetizer size). Fry in oil in wok or deep frypan. Serve immediately, or freeze and warm in oven before serving.

sauce

Apricot preserves	**Dijon mustard**
Plum preserves	**Peanut butter**
Soy sauce	

Combine amounts of ingredients to taste. Some prefer sauce rather sweet; others like it sharp.

ground-beef filling for egg rolls

1 pound ground beef
¼ cup margarine
4 cups very finely shredded cabbage
½ cup finely chopped scallion
1 cup finely chopped celery
2 cups fresh bean sprouts

¼ cup soy sauce
1 tablespoon sugar (or to taste)
Salt to taste
Freshly ground black pepper to taste

Brown beef in margarine until just browned. Add rest of ingredients; cook 5 minutes, stirring frequently. Adjust seasonings if necessary. Drain; cool. Use purchased egg-roll skins as a shortcut. Makes filling for about 24 egg rolls.

homemade chicken broth

Many Chinese recipes call for chicken broth. Canned broth is perfectly acceptable, but it is nice to use homemade broth at times. This can also be frozen.

1 stewing chicken, about 4 pounds
4 quarts water

Clean the chicken; remove excess yellow fat.

Bring water to boil in large pot. Place chicken in pot; cover. Let come to boil again; reduce heat to simmer. Cook chicken 3 to 4 hours, occasionally skimming off fat. Remove from heat; let broth cool. Discard skin and bones. Save meat for use in recipes. Store broth in covered glass jar in refrigerator. It will keep approximately 3 weeks if once a week it is brought to boil, cooled, and refrigerated again. If you prefer clear broth, strain before storing.

chinese chicken soup

1 soup chicken, about 4 pounds
2½ quarts water
2 small slices gingerroot

4 scallions
Salt to taste
1 tablespoon sherry (more if desired)

Combine chicken and water in pot; bring to boil. Add remaining ingredients. Cover; simmer over low heat about 3 hours or until chicken is tender. Remove chicken from soup; cut meat into small pieces. Strain soup; add chicken meat. Makes about 8 servings.

easy egg-drop soup

2 cans chicken broth, fat skimmed
1 can water
2 tablespoons cornstarch

4 tablespoons cold water
2 eggs, beaten slightly
2 tablespoons chopped scallions

Heat chicken broth and water, covered, until boiling.

Blend cornstarch with water. Slowly add to soup; turn off heat. Add eggs by pouring slowly into soup, stirring constantly.

Divide scallions into 4 individual soup bowls; add soup. Makes 4 servings.

salads and vegetables

ellen's marinated bean sprouts

This is an excellent salad to serve with meat or fish. It has a unique flavor. Try it for guests who like to sample something a little unusual. It's a favorite of ours!

1 pound fresh bean sprouts

marinade

3 tablespoons chopped scallion (green and white parts)
2 tablespoons sesame-seed oil

2 tablespoons soy sauce
1 tablespoon vodka
1 tablespoon vinegar

Place bean sprouts in colander; blanch. Immediately rinse with cold water; drain well.

Combine marinade ingredients in large bowl. Place bean sprouts in mixture; marinate at room temperature 1 hour. Refrigerate at least 3 hours before serving. Makes 4 servings.

cucumber salad

This can be made before you start to prepare the meal and stored in the refrigerator. Delicious!

1 large cucumber
2 tablespoons wine vinegar
2 tablespoons soy sauce

1 tablespoon sugar
1 tablespoon sesame oil
1 tablespoon sherry

Peel cucumber. Cut in half long way; scoop out seeds. Slice crosswise into very thin slices.

Mix together remaining ingredients; blend well. Pour over cucumber. slices. Makes 2 servings.

almond fried rice

1 large onion, chopped
1 green pepper, chopped
¼ cup butter
4 cups cooked rice
1 teaspoon garlic salt

¼ teaspoon freshly ground black pepper
¼ cup soy sauce
1 cup slivered toasted almonds

Cook onion and green pepper in butter until tender. Add remaining ingredients. Cook, stirring occasionally, 10 minutes. Makes 4 to 6 servings.

ginger rice

This is very tasty!

3 tablespoons oil
½ cup chopped scallions
2 tablespoons diced candied ginger
4 cups hot cooked rice

Heat oil in large skillet. Sauté scallions 1 minute. Add ginger and rice; stir lightly. Heat through. Makes 6 to 8 servings.

chinese-style green beans

These beans are *so* good!

2 tablespoons peanut oil
1 pound fresh green beans,
  washed, drained, cut into
  2-inch pieces

1 teaspoon salt
¼ teaspoon MSG
¼ cup cold water

Heat oil in skillet over high heat. Add beans; stir until coated with oil. Add salt and MSG; stir again just until ingredients are blended. Add water; cover pan. Reduce heat to medium; cook 10 minutes. Stir once. Cook, covered, until all liquid is absorbed. Makes 4 servings.

wok broccoli

1 pound fresh broccoli
2 tablespoons peanut oil
1 teaspoon sugar

½ teaspoon salt
½ cup water

Wash broccoli; break away small upper branches. Cut more-tender parts of stem into small crosswise slices.

Preheat oil in wok to 350°F. Add broccoli; stir-fry 1 minute. Add sugar, salt, and water; cover. Let broccoli steam 3 minutes. Cook another 5 minutes, stirring frequently. Makes 4 servings.

steamed eggplant

1 large eggplant, stem end
  sliced off, eggplant cut into
  6 wedges
Vegetable oil
1 large scallion, cut into
  2-inch pieces

2 tablespoons soy sauce
¼ teaspoon sugar
Dash of freshly ground black
  pepper
¼ teaspoon MSG

Steam eggplant, covered, 30 minutes over boiling water. Remove from heat.

Coat bottom and sides of preheated wok with oil. When hot, add scallion; quick-fry few seconds. Add eggplant, soy sauce, sugar, pepper, and MSG. Cook about 3 minutes, stirring constantly. Makes 4 servings.

delicious spinach

1 10-ounce package fresh
  spinach
2 tablespoons peanut oil
2 cloves garlic, crushed

½ teaspoon salt
½ teaspoon sugar
¼ teaspoon MSG

Wash and drain spinach; set aside.

Heat oil with garlic over medium-high heat. Add spinach; stir-fry until spinach is well coated with oil. Discard garlic. Add salt, sugar, and MSG; stir quickly. Cook 1 minute. Makes 2 servings.

desserts

chinese fruit salad

All the fruits in this recipe are available at Oriental food stores. Some may be available at your supermarket.

1 4-ounce jar ginger in syrup, drained
1 11-ounce can lichees in syrup, drained
1 8-ounce can kumquats, drained
1 20-ounce can longans, drained
1 12-ounce can water-lily roots, drained

1 16-ounce can mangos, drained
1 round watermelon, chilled, cut in half, meat and seeds removed, meat cut into balls or cubes
1 18-ounce can white nuts
1 lemon, sliced

Place ginger, lichees, kumquats, longans, lily roots, and mangos in large bowl; mix well. Chill until cold.

Cut slice off base of each watermelon half; place each half on serving dish. Place melon balls or cubes back into shells. Spoon mixed fruit on watermelon balls. Serve with nuts and lemon. Makes about 12 servings.

dessert fruit platter

The Chinese, as a rule, do not eat many sweets, either as dessert or as snacks. After a meal it would be very correct to offer a platter of fresh fruit, as shown. Here is an assortment of fruit, including mandarin oranges, strawberries, raspberries, bananas, grapes, honeydew melon, cherries, and peach slices, all attractively arranged. Guests always welcome a dessert of fresh fruit artistically presented. Delicious served with small pitcher of Fruit Dressing (see Index).

almond delight

1 envelope unflavored gelatin
3 tablespoons warm water
1 small can evaporated milk
1¼ cups cold water

6 tablespoons sugar
1 tablespoon almond extract
1 small can mandarin oranges
   (drain; reserve juice)

Dissolve gelatin in warm water.

Heat milk with cold water and sugar to just below boiling. Add gelatin mixture; cool. Add almond extract. Pour into square or rectangular glass dish; refrigerate to set. Cut into squares; float in syrup with mandarin oranges. Makes 4 servings.

orange syrup

¼ cup sugar
2 cups warm water

1 teaspoon almond extract
Juice from mandarin oranges

Dissolve sugar in water. Add almond extract and juice. Chill before serving. Serve in rice bowls. Very good!

chinese fruit salad

dessert fruit platter

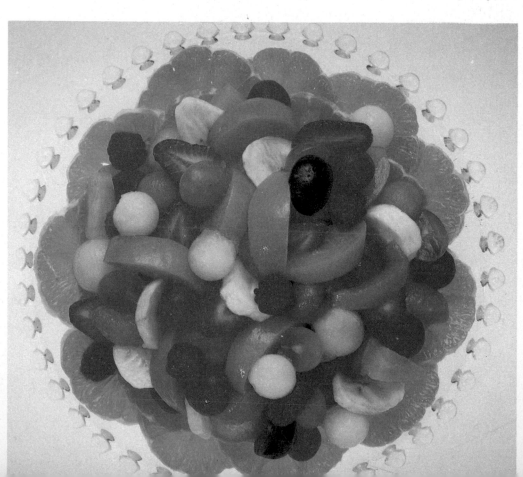

fruit dressing

This is delicious poured over any kind of fruit.

1 cup sugar
1 egg, well beaten
Juice and grated rind of 1 orange, 1 lime, and 1 lemon

Combine all ingredients in saucepan; blend well. Cook over medium heat, stirring constantly, until mixture comes to boil. Boil 1 minute; remove from heat. Cool; store in refrigerator in covered jar. Serve as accompaniment to dessert of fresh fruit. Makes about 1 pint.

fruit dressing

spiced kumquats

1 quart kumquats	**1 stick cinnamon**
3 cups sugar	**1 tablespoon whole cloves**
1 cup vinegar	**1 tablespoon whole allspice**

Wash and slit kumquats; place in pot. Cover with water; bring to boil. Cook 10 minutes; drain.

Combine sugar, vinegar, and 3 cups water in large saucepan; bring to boil.

Tie spices in small piece of muslin; drop into syrup. Cook 5 minutes. Add kumquats; cook 10 minutes. Discard spice bag. Let kumquats stand overnight. Bring to boil; cook until syrup is thick. Pack kumquats into hot sterilized jars; cover with syrup. Place lids on jars; screw bands tight. Process jars 10 minutes in boiling water. Makes about 3 pints.

pickled crab apples

4 pounds ripe crab apples	**½ tablespoon allspice**
4½ cups sugar	**1 1½-inch piece fresh**
2½ cups vinegar	** gingerroot**
2 cups water	**2 sticks cinnamon**
1 teaspoon salt	**Red food coloring (optional)**
½ tablespoon whole cloves	

Wash and rinse apples; drain. Remove stem end; prick apples with large needle.

Place sugar, vinegar, water, and salt in saucepan.

Tie spices in muslin bag; drop into pan. Cook, stirring constantly, until sugar dissolves. Add one layer of apples; boil gently 7 minutes.

Remove from pan; place in large bowl. Repeat until all crab apples are cooked; add few drops color to syrup. Pour syrup over crab apples; add spice bag. Cover; let stand in cool place 48 hours. Pack crab apples to within ½ inch of top of hot sterilized fruit jars.

Heat syrup to boiling; pour over crab apples. Place lids on jars; screw bands tight. Process pints and quarts 20 minutes in boiling water. Makes about 5 pints.

pickled figs

5 quarts firm ripe figs
1 cup soda
4 to 5 cups sugar
2½ cups vinegar
1 teaspoon salt
¼ teaspoon ground nutmeg
2 teaspoons whole cloves
2 teaspoons whole allspice
1 medium piece fresh
  gingerroot
3 sticks cinnamon
Green food coloring
  (optional)

Place figs in large bowl; sprinkle with soda. Add 6 quarts boiling water; let stand 5 minutes. Rinse figs thoroughly in cool water; drain.

Combine 2½ cups sugar and 2 quarts water in kettle; bring to boil. Add figs; cook 30 minutes or until tender. Add remaining sugar, vinegar, salt, and nutmeg.

Tie whole spices in bag; drop into syrup. Cook until figs are clear. Let stand in cool place overnight. Add coloring if desired. Pack figs to within ½ inch of top of pint jars.

Bring syrup to boil; pour over figs. Place lids on jars; screw bands tight. Process 15 minutes in boiling water. Makes about 6 pints.

pickled watermelon rind

5 pounds watermelon rind
1 tablespoon salt
8 teaspoons alum
9 cups sugar
1 quart cider vinegar
2 lemons, sliced thin
4 2-inch pieces cinnamon
  stick
2 teaspoons whole allspice
2 teaspoons whole cloves

Cut off and discard green and red portions from watermelon rind; leave only white inner rind. Cut into 1-inch pieces, about 4 quarts. Place rind in large stainless-steel or enamel pot. Add water to cover. Stir in salt; bring to boil. Reduce heat; simmer 20 minutes or until rind can be easily pierced with fork. Remove from heat. Stir in alum; cool. Cover; let stand 24 hours. Pour off water. Rinse; drain well. Add sugar, vinegar, lemon, and cinnamon sticks.

Tie allspice and cloves in cheesecloth bag. Add to rind mixture; mix well. Bring just to boil, stirring constantly. Remove from heat; cool, uncovered. Cover; let stand 24 hours.

Drain off syrup into large pan; bring just to boil. Pour over rind; cool. Cover; let stand 24 hours. Heat rind in syrup, but do not boil. Remove and discard spice bag. Pack rind and cinnamon in hot sterilized jars.

Heat syrup to boiling; fill jars with boiling syrup. Seal immediately. Store 4 weeks or longer before serving. Makes 4 quarts.

almond cookies

In China lard is used in almond cookies, but margarine makes a fine substitute. These cookies are very good.

1 cup shortening	3 tablespoons almond extract
1 cup sugar	4 tablespoons honey or corn
1 egg, beaten	syrup
3 cups sifted flour	1 cup blanched almonds
1½ teaspoons baking soda	

Cream together shortening and sugar. Add egg. Slowly add flour, baking soda, almond extract, and honey; blend until smooth. Take small piece of dough; roll into ball. Repeat until all dough is used. Flatten each ball to about ½ inch thick. Place almond in center of each. Bake on greased cookie sheet in preheated 375°F oven about 15 to 20 minutes. Makes about 4 dozen.

ginger ice cream

½ gallon vanilla ice cream
1 cup finely chopped candied ginger

Remove ice cream from carton; place in bowl. Allow to soften. Mix in candied ginger; spoon back into carton. Refreeze ice cream. Let stand in freezer at least 48 hours before serving, giving time for ginger flavor to penetrate ice cream. Makes about 12 servings.

glazed chestnuts

2 cups chestnuts
¾ cup honey
2 cups sugar

Place chestnuts in bowl with water to cover. Soak overnight; drain. Remove shells; dry on paper toweling.

Combine honey and sugar in saucepan. Cook over low heat 1 hour, stirring often. Add chestnuts; cook 2 hours, stirring often. Separate chestnuts on cookie sheets; cool. Makes about 24.

lichees

For a totally unique and delightful taste treat, try a dessert of lichees. This is a canned fruit in syrup, usually imported from Hong Kong. They can sometimes be purchased in your local supermarket, for sure at a Chinese food store. Try lichees mixed with other fruits; experiment with different combinations. One can of lichees makes approximately 4 servings.

lichees

index